Gifts of Genius

Gifts of Genius

TREASURES OF THE HUNTINGTON LIBRARY

by James Thorpe

THE HUNTINGTON LIBRARY · 1980

Above. The Exhibition Hall of the Huntington Library. The books and manuscripts which are the principal subjects of the essays in this book are on display in that Hall.

About the illustrations

All of the illustrations in this book are photographic facsimiles made directly from original sources in the collections of the Huntington Library and Art Gallery.

Contents

Library of Congress Catalog Card Number 80-80077
ISBN 0-87328-110-1

Introduction

WORKS OF GENIUS have the power to change the course of our lives. On rare occasions, they also change the course of civilization. The essays which make up this book explore some great human achievements that are gifts to the world from people of genius.

The Huntington is fortunate to have many treasures which are landmarks in our heritage from the past. This book focuses on some of those treasures which are on display in the Library Exhibition Hall.

They cover a period of six hundred years, from the latter fourteenth century to our own time. They represent many different kinds of human endeavor, but they share the quality of possessing great distinction. I approach them with pleasure, and I welcome the chance to offer, in an informal, personal way, some reflections on what I believe their importance to be.

The Huntington has, from its very beginning, been a place for research by scholars. The treasures on exhibition are only a tiny fraction of the body of rare books, manuscripts, prints, photographs, drawings, and art objects that make up the research collection. Scholars use this material in a multitude of ways in their unending search for deeper understanding. I share their delight in the availability of such a rich collection. It regularly produces the rare piece that the scholar would like to see, and sometimes the surprising item that suggests a wholly new way of thinking about the topic under consideration.

In these essays I have followed the scholar's way by turning for enlightenment to rare or unique material in the research collections. This book is thus a personal account of these treasures in the light of some of the primary resources of the Huntington Library. It is, most of all, an invitation to join in an exploration of important literary and historical milestones.

One of the great thrills of literary and historical research comes from actually handling those manuscripts and rare books. They give a sense of personal contact with the writer. You are dealing with his private notes, or studying the marginal comments that he put in one of his own books, or looking at his personal correspondence, or seeing the revisions he made in getting his work ready for publication, or going through his own photograph album, or reading the very first printing of one of his books, perhaps his own copy of it, or one that he gave to a friend.

This book includes many reproductions of rare and unique materials which are usually seen only by scholars. These photographic facsimiles were all made directly from the originals in the Huntington Library and Art Gallery, and a lot of them are printed in full color. I hope that these reproductions, in a form close to that of their originals, can convey a bit of the thrill that scholars feel while using the resources of a research library.

The creation of a research library is a complicated process. I have tried to tell the story of the history of some of the treasures and how they came to be here. In addition to these notes on the development of the Library, I have also given some hints about the dimensions of the holdings, of which the treasures may be the only visible part.

These essays were originally published as separate pamphlets. They are now collected, with minor revisions, as an introduction to some of the major treasures of the Huntington Library. And, through them, to some of the rare books and manuscripts which make up the research collection.

TREASURES OF THE HUNTINGTON LIBRARY

CHAUCER's *Canterbury Tales*

The Ellesmere Manuscript

About the illustrations

Over. Portrait of Chaucer, from the beginning of the Tale of Melibeus in the Ellesmere Manuscript, made about 1410.

Above. The tower exhibition case in which the Ellesmere Manuscript is displayed.

Facing page. Two pages of the Ellesmere Manuscript.

Portraits of the pilgrims. Of the 23 pilgrims, the portraits of 20 (from the Ellesmere Manuscript) are gathered together and printed on four successive pages; for each, a brief bit of Chaucer's characterization of that pilgrim is included. The other three — Chaucer, the Pardoner, and the Wife of Bath — are shown in the color facsimiles of portions of the pages on which their tales begin.

Chaucer's Canterbury Tales

The Ellesmere Manuscript

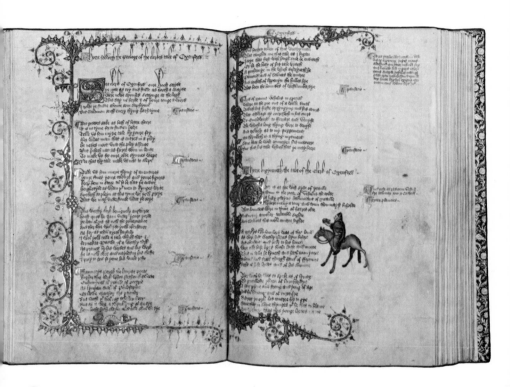

CHAUCER'S *Canterbury Tales* is the greatest English literary achievement of the entire medieval period. The Ellesmere Manuscript is a prime authority for the text of *The Canterbury Tales,* and it is thought to be the most beautiful literary manuscript of its period, or perhaps of any period. It is a noble heritage, both as a literary and as an artistic achievement. I am going to speak about *The Canterbury Tales* first as a literary work; next about Chaucer the man and the making of this manuscript; and finally about the Ellesmere Collection and how the Huntington Library happened to acquire that entire collection, including the Chaucer manuscript.

15

I

The Canterbury Tales as a whole consists of twenty-four stories, each with
its storyteller. It all took place in spring, long ago, as the familiar beginning tells us:

> Whan that Aprill with hise shoures soote
> The droghte of March hath perced to the roote,
> And bathed every veyne in swich licour,
> Of which vertu engendred is the flour;
> Whan Zephirus eek with his sweete breeth
> Inspired hath in every holt and heeth
> The tendre croppes, and the yonge sonne
> Hath in the Ram his half cours yronne,
> And smale foweles maken melodye,
> That slepen al the nyght with open eye
> (So priketh hem nature in hir corages);
> Thanne longen folk to goon on pilgrimages.

Spring is the time of rebirth in nature, and a similar spirit moves in man.
The people who longed to go on pilgrimages had some spring fever mixed
in with their piety. In springtime you might meet pilgrims almost anywhere. Chaucer tells us in the Prologue that he spent one April evening at
the Tabard Inn in the London suburb of Southwark, where he ran into
twenty-nine pilgrims, all going to visit the shrine of St. Thomas à Becket
at Canterbury. The thirty people decide to travel the sixty miles in a group
and tell stories en route, in competition for a prize — a free dinner at the
Tabard, on their return. The Host of the Tabard, named Harry Bailly, goes
along to act as judge in awarding the prize.

Here, for example, is one of the twenty-four stories. One night three
young friends went to a tavern and began to drink. They drank and
reveled and caroused and drank more and yet some more. Toward morning they heard a bell clinking in the street, signaling the passing of the
corpse of someone being carried to his grave. "Who's dead?", they asked.
"A close friend of yours," they were told, "who got very drunk last night.
While he was drunk, just sitting in his chair, there came a stealthy thief
men call Death, who smote your friend through the heart with his spear
and stole away without a word."

"What a rascal this Death is," they responded. "We'll fix him: we'll
kill him." So they held up their hands and took a solemn oath to be sworn
brothers to one another, and to kill Death.

They lurched out of the tavern and began to scour the countryside in
search of Death. Pretty soon they met a very old man so wrapped in a

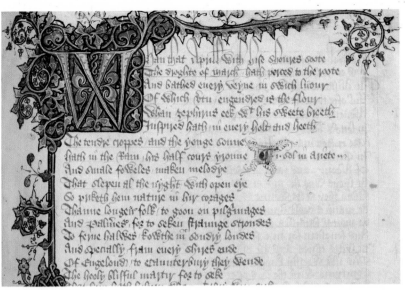

The opening of the General Prologue to *The Canterbury Tales: above* from the Elles-mere Manuscript; *below* from William Caxton's edition printed in Westminister (London) in 1478—this notable book is the first printing of *The Canterbury Tales,* or of any major English literary work.

cloak that they could see only his pale and withered face. The three friends bullied him because he was old and wrapped up — these faults seemed to them sufficient evidence that the old man was a rascal who deserved all the abuse they could pour on him.

The old man reacted very courteously, however, and apologized for being so old, explaining that Death wouldn't have him. With that, the three friends began to abuse him all the more and threatened to beat him up if he did not reveal to them where they could find Death.

"Oh," he said, "I just left him. Take that crooked path and when you get to an oak tree you'll find Death underneath it. He'll wait for you." So they rushed up the crooked path to the oak tree, expecting to find Death. But there they found eight bushels of gold coins. And the text says: "No longer then after Death they sought."

It took them only a few seconds to realize that the gold was theirs, their very own. How to get it home so that no one would know they had stolen it? Wait until night, of course, and then carry it away secretly, so that nobody would see it. That left a long day in front of them, and they would need food. So they drew lots, and the youngest one got the job of going into town and bringing bread and wine back to them, while the other two had the task of guarding their treasure.

As soon as the youngest one started for town, the other two sworn brothers began to wonder how they could manage to split the gold two ways instead of three. It did not take them long to settle on a scheme: when the youngest one returned, they would start a little playful wrestling match with him. Then, when they had him down, they would stab him to death with their daggers. That would save a third of the gold.

In the meantime, the youngest one was scheming how he might work it out so that he did not have to split the gold at all. Poison, that would do it. So he bought the bread and the wine and three bottles, and he went to an apothecary shop. He asked the apothecary to sell him some poison to kill the rats and the skunks that were after his chickens. He put this potion — for rats and skunks — into two of his bottles, leaving the third for himself, and went back down the crooked path to the oak tree where his fellows were waiting for him.

They were indeed waiting for him. They stabbed him and slew him, and then they sat down to make merry with his bread and wine. They chose a bottle with poison in it, and it was truly their Last Supper. There they lay, all three, under the oak tree, by the piles of gold. They had succeeded in finding Death before nightfall.

That is the story of "The Pardoner's Tale" in *The Canterbury Tales*. It is a very good story, interesting and exciting in the way it is told, with a slightly horrifying fascination like a Dance of Death, and full of twists

The beginning of the Pardoner's Tale, with a portrait of the Pardoner, from the Ellesmere Manuscript.

and ironies. Of course no work of art can be judged on the basis of a report, and hearing about a work of art is an entirely different experience from coming in contact with the work of art itself. A literary work must be read or heard or seen, a visual work must be looked at, music must be listened to.

So I cannot, on the basis of this retelling, demonstrate that "The Pardoner's Tale" is an important work of art, but perhaps I can offer some hint as to what I think the contemporary reader made of it. Basically and obviously, an allegory on the idea that the love of money is the root of all evil. The heart of John Huston's classic movie, "The Treasure of the Sierra Madre," with Humphrey Bogart, is a simplified version of the same avarice theme that leads to death in "The Pardoner's Tale." Three men go out into the mountains of Mexico prospecting for gold, and they find it. The movie shows the increasing suspicion of each toward the others, and their increasing avarice; it ends as it must — the tragic story of death that comes from their avarice and their lack of charity.

The action of "The Pardoner's Tale" turns on the line "No longer then after Death they sought," when they discover the treasure of gold coins. That line seems to be saying that they forget their search after Death, but

19

what it is actually saying is that they no longer have to seek because they have in fact found Death, masquerading as gold coins.

An interesting parallel about finding Death is in a Somerset Maugham story which John O'Hara quotes as the epigraph to "Appointment in Samarra." It goes this way. In the city of Baghdad, a servant came to his master and told him that he had just encountered Death in the marketplace, and that Death had frightened him exceedingly by the way he looked at him. The servant asked for the loan of the master's horse so that he might flee to Samarra where Death could not find him. Certainly, said the master, and off rode the servant. The master then went himself to the marketplace and looked up Death. "What do you mean, frightening my servant by looking so menacingly at him?" Death replied: "I didn't look menacingly at him. I was simply surprised to see him here in Baghdad, when he and I have an appointment together tonight, in Samarra."

In Chaucer's time, now 600 years in the past, I believe that "The Pardoner's Tale" would have been understood by most readers in Christian terms. We are enjoined to search for eternal life and practice charity, but the revelers search for death and practice selfishness. What happens at the end of the story is not only their physical death, but also — in the unworthy celebration of the Holy Communion with their bread and wine — their spiritual death as well.

Sometimes we may feel that we are much more sophisticated than people who lived a long time ago, that they were relatively simpleminded and

The procession of Chaucer's pilgrims on the way to Canterbury as designed and engraved by William Blake in 1810. The original is about three feet long and one foot

that we see deeper into the mystery of things. If we are ever tempted to take that view, "The Pardoner's Tale" (as a sample of *The Canterbury Tales* as a whole) can serve as an antidote (or perhaps as an emetic) to such poison of cultural pride before it does us serious harm.

Chaucer makes a special point of vividly describing the pilgrims who tell *The Canterbury Tales*. The Pardoner — a preacher who solicits offerings and grants indulgences — is a perversion of his own tale: he is muddled by drink while he is telling his story of the three drunken revelers who find death, he is guilty of the avarice his story condemns, and he knows that his relics and pardons are fakes. He has a loud, high-pitched voice, and there are other suggestions (he cannot grow a beard, for example) that he is lacking in masculinity. The pilgrims come across like real people; they are often as interesting as their stories, and our understanding of the tales is enriched by knowing the pilgrims and their relation to their own stories and to one another.

Chaucer included in *The Canterbury Tales* almost every kind of story there was — romance, folktale, saint's legend, parody, beast fable, comedy, sermon, bawdy jest, and the rest. He even includes a Women's Lib story, in the form of "The Wife of Bath's Tale." The Wife of Bath has run through five husbands; she managed to keep the upper hand with each of them, and she is now looking for a sixth.

Her story is about a knight who was condemned to death but offered a pardon if he could, within a year, discover what it is that women most

high. Blake portrayed the pilgrims as representing the inner qualities of all types of people on their journey through life.

desire. The knight cannot hit on a satisfactory solution, and the very end of the year breathes upon him. Then an ugly old hag offers to tell him the answer, on one condition — that he will later perform any single deed that she asks him to do. He agrees, and she tells him the answer — that women most desire to have mastery over their husbands. The answer is right, he gets his pardon, and the old hag turns up to have him fulfill the condition. It is that he marry her. He almost faints at the thought, but no matter how much he argues or what alternatives he offers, he has to go through with it, like a proper knight. She tells him all the advantages of having an ugly, old wife — no fear of jealousy, no competition from other men, and so forth. But at last she offers him a choice: take her old and ugly but absolutely faithful; or take her young and beautiful but of doubtful fidelity. The knight, having learned his lesson well, says, "You decide; whichever you say will be best." Thus, when he has given her mastery over him, she gives herself to him as young and beautiful *and* absolutely faithful.

Since Chaucer is also one of the pilgrims, he portrays himself as being called on to tell a tale. His story gives us a clue about him, or at least about how he wanted himself seen. After Harry Bailly has teased him for his plumpness and for keeping his eyes on the ground, Chaucer apologetically commences his "Tale of Sir Thopas," which seems to be a solemn story in verse of knight-errantry but is really a comic burlesque. Bailly, who takes it seriously, cannot tolerate it. "No more of this, for God's sake," he cries out, and Chaucer then tells a long, dull story in prose, "The Tale of Melibeus," one of the least memorable tales in the entire collection. Most of us try to cast ourselves in an attractive role, and I imagine that few would willingly choose to present themselves, as Chaucer did himself, in the pose of looking ridiculous and dull.

Why, one may ask, is *The Canterbury Tales* such an important achievement? Why is it worth learning Middle English — the form of English used in Chaucer's time, only roughly comprehensible today without special study — if one were to do no more with it than read *The Canterbury Tales*? For many reasons, of course, including the ones that make all great literary works of value to us. In particular, *The Canterbury Tales* reveals us to ourselves by its rich portrayal of the kinds of people we are and of the ways we act. It shows us as sometimes wise and sometimes foolish and sometimes a little of each, dignified and vulgar, magnanimous and self-serving, solemn and ridiculous, and as varied as we can be. It appeals to — and helps us to develop — our sense of fun, of fairness, of kindness, of wonder, of beauty, and other qualities that go to make us mature human beings. *The Canterbury Tales* is also a great pleasure to read.

Geoffrey Chaucer died in 1400, half a century before the beginning of printing, at the age of about sixty. He was a man of high position in his own time. He was in the army which invaded France in 1359 and was taken prisoner but soon ransomed. He held various posts of importance at court, he was sent on numerous diplomatic missions to the Continent in the 1470s (including at least two journeys to Italy and secret service work in Flanders), he was Controller of Customs for the Port of London, he was a Member of Parliament in 1386, and he was for several years the supervisor of construction for various public buildings (including the Tower of London and St. George's Chapel, Windsor) and royal residences. He lived in a world of violence: he was robbed two or three times within a period of four days in 1390, and on one of those occasions he was beaten up. He wrote many important literary works (such as "The Book of the Duchess," "Troilus and Criseyde," and "The Legend of Good Women") as well as such prose as his translation of Boethius. In recognition of his importance, he was buried in Westminster Abbey.

Chaucer wrote *The Canterbury Tales* in the last years of his life. He began the writing about 1387, but he never completed the ambitious plan of having each pilgrim tell four tales, two on the way to Canterbury and two on the way home. Only twenty-three of the thirty pilgrims get a chance to tell a story, and one tale by the Pardoner is probably more effective than two or three or four. In any event, *The Canterbury Tales* is sufficiently complete to be judged a remarkable achievement. It quickly became a famous work, much circulated in manuscript. About 1410, somebody decided to have a really deluxe manuscript made of it, one that would be the most authentic and the most beautiful of any in existence. Thus began the work of creating our manuscript.

It was apparently made in or around London, very likely in a commercial scriptorium, which was a shop in which scribes made copies of manuscripts to order. (This was, remember, before the invention of printing in Europe, and "books" had to be written by hand; it was also after the time when most copying was done in monasteries.) The manuscript was, in any event, a piece of professional work by a professional scribe.

The job of writing was hard work, and scribes often complained about their lot. One wrote that

> Mine handys gin to fainte
> My wit to dullen, and mine eyen to blente.

Even the pen — a quill, which the scribe had to cut frequently in order to keep it sharp — would begin to blot:

And in my book maketh many a spot,
Meaning thereby that for the beste
Were for us both a while to reste,
Till that my wit and also he
Might by some craft repaired be.

We can make a pretty accurate reconstruction of how our manuscript was made. Copying the text was altogether the work of one scribe, who sat at his desk day after day. Experts can identify some of the places where he stopped to sharpen his quill or stir his ink, even where he recommenced his work after an interruption like the end of a day. We do not know his name, but scholars who specialize in early handwriting (paleographers) have identified one other manuscript (in the National Library of Wales) which they feel confident is also his work.

The scribe (if he followed the usual practice) did not work on a flat table, but at a sloping desk so that his work was more or less at eye level. He had his copy, which had been carefully (and expertly) corrected before it was given to him, and a booklet — called a quire — of eight blank leaves of vellum, sixteen pages, folded together, which he began to fill up with his writing. Our manuscript required twenty-nine quires for its 232 leaves of vellum, or 464 pages.

The vellum was made from either calfskin or sheepskin. A skin was prepared by being soaked in a caustic lime solution, scraped and shaved on both sides to an even thinness, rubbed smooth with pumice, and stretched till completely dry. Then it was cut to size. The largest calfskins were said to measure about two feet by three feet after they had been prepared for use. Our manuscript, being exceptionally large, is probably calfskin; one of the largest calfskins would have done well to make four of its leaves. Thus our manuscript took at least fifty-eight of the largest skins — or more, if smaller skins were used — and it was, because of the price of vellum, very expensive to produce.

The scribe first pricked holes with an awl as a guide to ruling the lines. As this manuscript was to have forty-eight lines of text to the page, the scribe made forty-eight pricks in the inner and outer edges of each leaf and connected them with a line, which was his guide for writing the text of that line. (Both sides of the vellum were ruled from one set of prick-marks, and sometimes several leaves were pricked at once.) Then the scribe set forth writing, slowly, in a large clear book hand of the kind then used for writing deluxe books in English.

The making of manuscripts was almost on an assembly-line basis. When the scribe had finished a quire, he passed it over to the corrector, who compared it with the copy and corrected any mistakes he saw. Then the quire was passed on to the rubricator, who did the pen ornamentation in red and blue ink. Then the illuminator added the gold work and the painting on border pages. "Illumination" literally means lightened, especially by the use of gold, though other colors were also used; similarly, "rubrication" literally and traditionally meant to set off letters or parts of the text by the use of red, but again other colors different from the context were also used.

A full-color plate in this essay reproduces one sample page of the manuscript. Although the sample page had to be reduced to one-fourth of the size of the manuscript, I hope that it still conveys some sense of the original. (The dimensions of the original are a stately 15¾″ by 11⅛″, while the size of this pamphlet is approximately 9″ by 6″.) The decorations include borders, large initials, and paragraph marks. The borders fill three margins with stylized sprays and branches, leaves, and flowers which are in gold and in several other colors. The large initials, of which we have one on the sample page, are at the beginning of each tale: they are mostly in pink and blue on a gold ground. Some seventy-one pages were given the full decorative treatment. The paragraph marks, of which you can see perhaps half a dozen in the text on the sample, brighten the entire manuscript, sometimes with twenty-five or more on a single page.

When the writing and the decorating were finished, artists then painted the portraits of the pilgrims in the margins. There are twenty-three portraits in the manuscript, one of each pilgrim who tells a tale. All are portrayed on horseback, as if they were riding to Canterbury, and each appears at the beginning of his tale. The artists must have read the tales with care — or been given exact instructions by some knowledgeable person — because the details they use in depicting the pilgrims are in keeping with Chaucer's description of them. The Miller, for example, is shown blowing on his bagpipe, just as he did (according to the text) as the pilgrims rode out of London; and his thumb is gold, to fulfill the proverbial (but ironic) notion of an honest miller. These are among the very earliest examples of English portrait paintings, most of which are to be found in manuscripts. It was not until more than a century later that it became usual for English portrait paintings to be done separately, either in miniature form or (as we more commonly think of paintings) on wood or canvas. One or two other manuscripts of *The Canterbury Tales* contain portraits of some of the pilgrims, but no other extant manuscript has a complete set of portraits.

The portrait on the color plate in this essay is the most famous (and the largest) one of all those in this manuscript, the portrait of Chaucer himself, just beginning to tell his "Tale of Melibeus." With his left index finger he is pointing to the beginning of his tale. As the writing is unfamiliar and small, I will transcribe a few lines. "Heere bigynneth Chaucers tale of

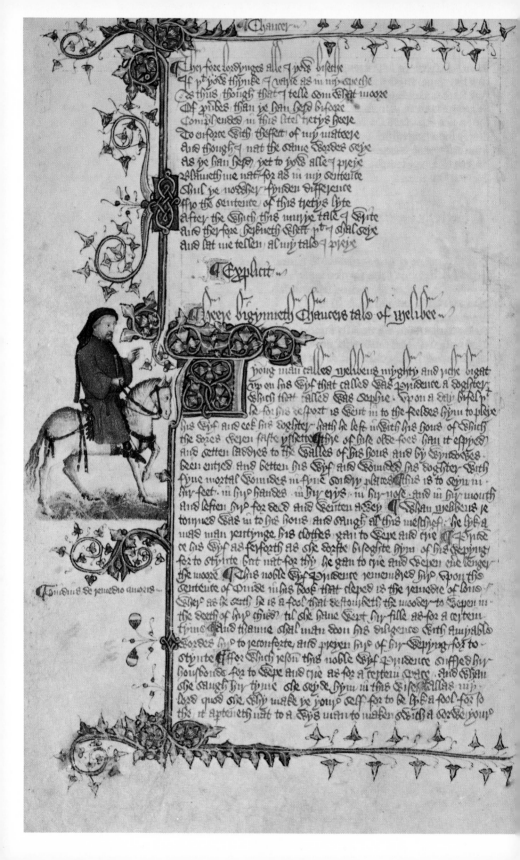

Melibee," it starts out, in bold letters. Then the large initial letter, a capital "A," much decorated in color. The tale, in prose, commences:

> A yong man called Melibeus myghty and riche bigat
> upon his wyf that called was Prudence a doghter
> which that called was Sophie. Upon a day bifel that
> he for his desport is went in to the feeldes hym to pleye.

While he was gone, his wife and daughter were beaten up, and the tale is a debate as to whether Melibeus should be vengeful or forgiving.

The portrait of Chaucer also appears, in larger form, at the front of this essay. (The other pilgrims are shown later.) With his right hand, Chaucer is holding the reins of his horse. He wears a gown and a headdress; he has a mustache, a two-pointed beard, a largish nose, and his hair covers half his ear. The draftsmanship is rather crude, particularly in the disproportion between the upper and lower parts of his body, and the disproportion between man and horse. (It is commonly thought that our portrait was copied from a bust-portrait which was done from life but is no longer extant; according to this idea, the artist spoiled the proportions while adding legs and a horse.) But no matter. We should cherish it as the earliest surviving portrait of Chaucer, and remember that it was painted into the manuscript about 1410. Another portrait of Chaucer, painted about 1412 and thought to be from the same bust-portrait, is contained in a manuscript of a poem by Hoccleve, who had the portrait included as a testimonial to his friend Chaucer and who personally verified the likeness; it is remarkably similar to the portrait in our manuscript.

The portraits of the pilgrims appear to be the work of either three or four artists. One artist painted the portrait of Chaucer and of no other pilgrim. The other five pilgrims whose horses are walking on a patch of grass — the Nun's Priest, the Canon's Yeoman, the Second Nun, the Manciple, and the Monk — are thought to have been painted by one artist. The other eighteen portraits are thought to have been done either by one or by two other artists.

An interesting sidelight about the portrait work comes from noticing that three of the horses — those ridden by the Franklin, the Shipman, and the Squire — were first traced with a stylus from a medieval copybook to leave an outline for the artist to follow; the indentation in the vellum is still visible in the manuscript. Then, presumably, the rider was added to the horse by freehand. It is possible that other figures, including Chaucer's, were prepared in the same way. If that were the case, the artist may have spoiled the proportions in the portrait of Chaucer by adding a man to a horse rather than a horse to a man.

THE SUMMONER
Of his visage children were aferd.

THE CLERK OF OXFORD
And gladly wolde he lerne and gladly teche.

THE KNIGHT
He was a verray, parfit, gentil knyght.

THE MILLER
He was short-sholdred, brood, a thikke knarre.

THE PRIORESS
Ful weel she soong the service dyvyne,
Entuned in her nose ful semely.

THE NUN'S PRIEST
See, whiche braunes hath this gentil preest,
So gret a nekke, and swich a large breest!

THE SQUIRE
He was fressh as is the month of May.

THE FRANKLIN
To lyven in delit was evere his wone.

THE REEVE
A sclendre colerik man.

THE COOK
For blankmanger, that made he with the beste.

THE SECOND NUN
Another Nonne with hire hadde she,
That was hir chapeleyne.

THE CANON'S YEOMAN
I am so used in the [alchemist's] fyr to blowe
That it hath chaunged my colour, I trowe.

The pilgrims cover a wide range of the society of Chaucer's time. The pilgrim who stands highest in the social order of the time is the Knight, and the scale of his portrait is appropriately large; even his horse is massive and aggressive, with eyes that look as if the horse wishes to spy out and destroy an enemy in combat. The Knight's tale is a long romance of chivalry which culminates in a tournament in which the winner is supposed to get the girl. The Squire, the Knight's son, is a dashing young man

THE MAN OF LAW
Nowher so bisy a man as he ther nas,
And yet he seemed bisier than he was.

THE FRIAR
Somwhat he lipsed, for his wantownesse
To make his English sweete upon his tonge.

THE MERCHANT
His resons he spak ful solemnpnely,
Sowynge alwey th'encrees of his wynnyng.

THE PHYSICIAN
For gold in phisik is a cordial
Therefore he lovede gold in special.

wearing (as the text says) a short coat with long, wide sleeves and as covered with flowers as a meadow, on a horse literally rearing to go; the Squire tells a romantic story (unfortunately fragmentary) about three objects with magical powers, a brass steed, a mirror, and a gold ring. Almost a third of the pilgrims are officials of the Church: the Pardoner, for example, is wearing a long red coat, and his red hat has on it the talisman of a veronica (the supposed face of Jesus, from the image on St. Veronica's

THE SHIPMAN
Of nyce conscience took he no keep.

THE MONK AND HIS GREYHOUNDS
Grehoundes he hadde as swift as fowel in flight.

THE PARSON
To drawen folk to hevene by fairnesse,
By good ensample, this was his bisynesse.

THE MANCIPLE [OF AN INN OF COURT]
Now is nat that of God a ful fair grace
That swich a lewed mannes wit shal pace
The wisdom of an heep of lerned men?

31

handkerchief); he is carrying a large cross (presumably of cheap metal, with imitation gems in it), and his long yellow curls hang down below his shoulders. The red-faced Wife of Bath has a riding skirt around her ample hips, spurs on her feet, a hat with a brim as wide as a shield, a wimple over her head and hair. The portraits of the pilgrims are all of special interest while one is reading their tales.

III

The early history of our manuscript is a little obscure. It seems to have belonged, for some time in the fifteenth and sixteenth centuries, to the Earls of Oxford. I want to speak now, however, of its three hundred years in the Ellesmere Collection and its acquisition for the Huntington Library.

The Ellesmere Collection was founded by Sir Thomas Egerton, in the latter part of the sixteenth century, during the reign of Queen Elizabeth. It is the oldest large family library in England. Egerton's life began inauspiciously enough, as he was the illegitimate child of a country maidservant. He became a lawyer, however, and he early attracted the attention of Queen Elizabeth, who heard him plead a case. With her favor, his rise in the world was rapid. He was made Solicitor General when he was forty-one, was knighted, and was made Lord Keeper of the Great Seal. He continued in high office under King James I as Lord Chancellor and was made Baron Ellesmere. In the process, he accumulated a great many landed estates, and a great deal of money.

He was a lover of books and manuscripts, and he accumulated a great many of them also. He had a Traveling Library, which consisted of fortyfour volumes in a case two feet long, one foot wide, and five inches high.

Whenever he was away from home — a great part of the time — he took the Traveling Library with him. It is now in the Huntington Library and usually on display.

He was closely associated with a good many literary people. John Donne was his secretary, for example, and he befriended Francis Bacon and helped him in adversity. His library contained many presentation copies and many dedication copies from both grateful and aspiring writers.

His son, who became the first Earl of Bridgewater, was the one for whom Milton wrote *Comus*, with the Earl's children taking principal parts at its first performance in 1634 at their Ludlow Castle. It is thought that our Chaucer manuscript came into the Ellesmere Collection during this Earl's lifetime, perhaps by 1620. And so it continued for hundreds of years, safe from the vandalism that defaced or destroyed so many early manuscripts, particularly the beautiful ones with paintings in them. In 1803 the Ellesmere Collection was moved to a family property in London, Bridgewater House.

When the third Earl of Ellesmere died, in 1914, his successor decided to sell the entire collection in order to pay the large death duties.

Here is where Henry E. Huntington enters the story. In December 1916 the London auction firm of Sotheby, Wilkinson & Hodge issued a catalog entitled as follows: "Description of the Renowned Library at Bridgewater House, London. The Property of The Right Hon. The Earl of Ellesmere. With A Detailed Catalogue of Some of the More Valuable among the Magnificent Illuminated Manuscripts and Printed Books Composing It."

The introduction to the catalog says that "Perhaps the most notable item is the superb Ellesmere Chaucer (the Canterbury Tales) written shortly after the Poet's death, and beautifully illuminated and containing the unique picture of the Poet." Item number 1 in the catalog is "The Ellesmere Chaucer." The comment on it begins as follows:

> **** A superb manuscript of the highest possible importance. With the possible exception of Milton's Autograph MSS. in the Library of Trinity College, Cambridge, this manuscript is unquestionably the greatest monument of English literature in the world.

One would think that the language of praise could no further go. And yet the catalog continues, now quoting scholars: "Professor W. W. Skeat used the text of this manuscript as the basis of his edition of The Canterbury Tales in the 'Complete Works of Chaucer,' Oxford, Clarendon Press, and refers to it in his Introduction as 'THE FINEST AND BEST OF ALL THE MSS. NOW EXTANT.' . . . Professor Schlegel also mentions that this is the most important of all English MSS. to scholars, on account of the fine middle-English text."

Surely this would be enough to make the mouth of any book collector begin to water. I imagine that Mr. Huntington became restless from the itch of acquisitiveness, even before reading about the Caxtons, the Shakespeare quartos and folios, the Eliot Indian Bible, the early Americana, and so forth.

George D. Smith, the book dealer who acted as agent for Mr. Huntington during this period, was in New York at the time. Unfortunately for us, so was Mr. Huntington, with the result that we do not have any letters between them on the subject. A lot of discussion and negotiation must have gone on between December 1916 and February 1917, however. The collection was never offered for public sale. On February 21 a purchase agreement was prepared, and on February 27, 1917 a contract was signed for the purchase. It took the form of a letter to Messrs Sotheby, Wilkinson & Hodge as follows:

```
Messrs Sotheby Wilkinson & Hodge

    Dear Sirs

                I hereby confirm the purchase by me of the
Library,known as the "Bridgewater Library" of the Right
Hon. The Earl of Ellesmere,London,as described in the
printed Catalogue and check list of said Library for the
sum of one million dollars ($1,000,000.00) in United States
Coin or its equivalent,payable as follows:
```

The letter then gives the terms for paying this round sum of one million dollars. As it happened, no "United States Coin" was to change hands, but four installments of cash and promissory notes would clear it up. At least Mr. Huntington did not offer to pay the bill with bonds or real estate, taken at his own valuation, which he frequently did. At about this same time he was treating with a book dealer in San Francisco for the purchase of a collection of Californiana, and they readily agreed on the price of $25,000. "If I could exchange real estate here for the books," wrote Mr. Huntington to him, "I think I might be inclined to take them. If not, I will return the catalogue." A compromise resulted in the payment of fifteen Pacific Electric Railway Refunding 5 percent bonds, and $10,000 worth of real estate, sight unseen.

The news of the purchase of the Bridgewater Library — or the Ellesmere Collection, as it was commonly called in England — did not reach the press for some time. When it did, however, it made a considerable splash. The story in the *New York Times* for May 21, 1917 had four headlines, the first of which was "Rare Literary Gems for H. E. Huntington," and the second was "Ellesmere Chaucer Ranks with Milton Manuscripts as Greatest Survival of Its Kind." The story quoted virtually all of the comment from the Sotheby catalog about the Ellesmere Chaucer — a practice which I understand to be a recognized shortcut for reporters.

Other newspapers and magazines played the same tune. The *New York Evening Post* reported that Mr. Huntington now had "the most famous manuscript of English literature, if not of any literature in the world, Chaucer's 'Canterbury Tales.' " The *New York Evening Sun* proclaimed that "the superb vellum manuscript of the 'Canterbury Tales', illuminated a few years after Chaucer's death, is regarded as the greatest literary monument of English literature." The printed reports commonly say something like this: "Most important of all manuscripts is the celebrated Ellesmere Chaucer, written within a few years of Chaucer's death. This is the basis of all the printed editions of his 'Canterbury Tales.' "

Of course there is a good deal of hyperbole involved in these statements. But the question "What is the most famous manuscript?" is different from the question "What is truth?" Jesting Pilate would not stay for an answer to the latter question. But if enough people say with enough force — and without contradiction — that the Ellesmere Chaucer is the most famous manuscript of them all, then that mirror on the wall which is public opinion will in time agree. A single memorable opinion, frequently reiterated, sometimes obscures other interesting matters. Such as that the Bridgewater Library that Mr. Huntington acquired included many, many fascinating and significant treasures: it consisted of some 4,400 printed books in all (many of them very rare), and about 14,500 manuscripts (of which 2,500 are manuscripts of plays).

This acquisition was neither the first nor the last of the great Huntington acquisitions of books and manuscripts. In the six years preceding, he had bought six major collections: the E. Dwight Church Collection in 1911 for $1,200,000, the Beverly Chew Library in 1912 for $500,000, Hoe Library books in 1912 for $500,000, the Duke of Devonshire Library in 1914 for $1,000,000, the Frederick R. Halsey Library in 1915 for $750,000, and the Britwell Court Americana in 1916 for $350,000. There were many other purchases for $100,000 or less during the same period. (In the remaining ten years of Mr. Huntington's life, he bought many further collections; the Huntington Library continues to grow, and it now has several times as many books as it did when Mr. Huntington died in 1927.)

Though it would be hard to maintain that the Bridgewater Library led all earlier acquisitions in importance, it seems to have had special significance in the public mind. Soon thereafter the Huntington Library begins to be treated with a new kind of esteem, as if it had been promoted to a class all by itself. One example is a long story in the *New York Times* magazine section for May 27, 1917. The story is headed "Huntington Now the Premier Book Collector." It begins as follows: "To Henry E. Huntington belongs, par excellence, the title of Prince of Book Collectors.

With books of Kings and Queens in his library, imprints from the first presses of Gutenberg, Fust, Caxton, and other worthies who were pioneers in making literature accessible to the man in the street instead of only to the student in the cloister, original editions of the great dramatists and masters of the English tongue in poetry and fiction, and countless other rarities which have contributed to the world's knowledge of everything under the sun, Mr. Huntington takes his place as the first bibliophile in the land."

The story goes on to explain why he has *now* taken this place. "Mr. Huntington attained the climax of distinction among book collectors by his acquisition a few days ago for $1,00,000 of the Bridgewater Library, which has been renowned in England from the days of Queen Elizabeth." The story continues, inevitably, with this set sentence: "The choicest treasure in the Bridgewater collection is the superb manuscript on vellum of the 'Canterbury Tales,' known as the 'Ellesmere Chaucer.' "

It does not appear that Mr. Huntington was much altered by this increase in esteem. Soon afterward, a reporter wrote the following account of an interview with him: "In manner he is soft voiced and shy almost to the point of apparent timidity in the presence of strangers. Six feet in height, broad shouldered as an athlete, his keen eyes sparkling with intensive vision, his is a figure not soon to be forgotten."

Mr. Huntington showed the reporter various rarities, such as the Gutenberg Bible and the Washington Genealogy, and then picked up the Ellesmere Chaucer. Here is the way his visitor reported it: " 'See, this is the first hand-illuminated manuscript of the "Canterbury Tales," ' said the owner of what is considered the supreme masterpiece of rare books, 'and on this page, as you see, is the only known genuine portrait of Chaucer, riding on his little nag.' "

Obviously, he opened the manuscript to the very page which is reproduced in the course of this essay, the page to which it often stands open on exhibition. As a symbol for the half a million printed books and five million manuscripts in the Huntington Library, the Ellesmere Chaucer stands open as an invitation to generations of visitors and generations of scholars to come and enjoy and learn from the treasures of this institution.

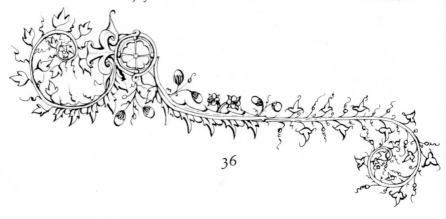

THE GUTENBERG BIBLE

Incipit liber bresith quē nos genesim
dicim⁹. In principio creauit deus celū
et terram. Terra autem erat inanis et
vacua: et tenebre erāt sup facie abissi:
et spūs dūi ferebat sup aquas. Dixitq;
deus. Fiat lux. Et facta ē lux. Et vidit
deus lucem cp esser bona: z diuisit lucē
a tenebris: appellauitq; lucem diem z
tenebras noctā. Factūq; est vespe et
mane dies vnus. Dixit qq; deus. Fiat
firmamentū in medio aquarū: z diui-
dat aquas ab aquis. Et fecit deus firmamentū: diuisitq; aquas que erāt
sub firmamento ab hijs q̄ erant sup
firmamentū: et factū ē ita. Vocauitq;
deus firmamentū celū: z factū ē vespe
et mane dies secūd⁹. Dixit vero deus.
Congregent aque que sub celo sūt in
locū vnū z appareat arida. Et factū ē
ita. Et vocauit deus aridam terram:
congregacioesq; aquaꝝ appellauit
maria. Et vidit deus cp esser bonū: et
ait. Germinet terra herbā virentem et
facientē semen: z lignū pomiferū faciēs
fructū iuxta genus suū: cui⁹ semen in
semetipso sit sup terrā. Et factū ē ita. Et
protulit terra herbā virentē z facientē
semē iuxta genus suū: lignūq; faciēs
fructū z habes vnūqdq; sementē sedm
speciē suā. Et vidit deus cp esser bonū:
et factū est vespe et mane dies tercius.
Dixitq; autē deus. Fiant luminaria
in firmamēto celi z diuidāt diem ac
noctem: z sint in signa z tpa et dies z
annos: ut luceāt in firmamēto celi et
illuminēt terrā. Et factū ē ita. Fecitq;
deus duo luminaria magna: luminare
maius ut presser diei et luminare min⁹
ut presser nocti z stellas: z posuit eas in
firmamēto celi ut lucerent sup terrā:

pessent diei ac nocti: z diuiderent lucē
ac tenebras. Et vidit deus cp esser bonū:
et factū ē vespe z mane dies quartus.
Dixit etia deus. Producāt aque reptile
anime viuentis z volatile super terrā
sub firmamēto celi. Creauitq; deus cete
grandia et omne aiam viuentē atq;
motabilē quā pduxerāt aque ī species
suas: z omne volatile sedm genⁱ suū.
Et vidit deus cp esser bonū: benedixitq;
eis dicens. Crescite z multiplicamini z
replete aquas maris: auesq; multipli-
cent sup terrā. Et factū ē vespe z mane
dies quintus. Dixit quoq; deus. Pro-
ducat terra aiam viuentē in genre suo:
iumenta z reptilia z bestias terre sedm
species suas. Factūq; ē ita. Et fecit de⁹
bestias terre iuxta species suas: iumenta z omne reptile terre ī genere suo. Et
vidit deus cp esser bonū: et ait. Facia-
mus hoiem ad ymagine z similitudinē
nostrā: z presit piscibz maris: et volatilibz celi z bestijs vniuerseq; terre: omni-
q; reptili qd mouetur ī terra. Et creauit
deus hoiem ad ymagine z similitudinē
suā: ad ymagine dei creauit illū: ma-
sculū z feminā creauit eos. Benedixit-
q; illis deus: z ait. Crescite z multiplicamini z replete terrā: z sbicite eā: et dūa-
mini piscibz maris: et volatilibz celi:
et vniuersis animātibz que mouent
sup terrā. Dixitq; deus. Ecce dedi vobis
omne herbā afferentē semen sup terrā:
et vniūsa ligna que hūt in semetipis
sementē generis sui: ut sint vobis ī esca:
z cunctis aiantibz terre: omniq; volucri
celi z vniuersis q mouetur in terra: z ī
quibz est anima viuēs: ut habeāt ad
vescendū. Et factū est ita. Viditq; deus
cuncta que fecerat: z erāt valde bona.

About the illustrations

Over. The first page of the Book of Genesis in the Gutenberg Bible, showing the creation. About one-fourth of the size of the original.

Above. The earliest portrait of John Gutenberg. This engraving, presumably an imaginary likeness, shows a man with a forked beard and a furred cap, with a die for twelve letters of the alphabet in his left hand. It first appeared in a book by André Thevet, Paris, 1584.

The Gutenberg Bible
Landmark in Learning

RARELY HAS FAME ever been so well placed as that which surrounds the Gutenberg Bible. This noble book, which appeared about 1455, has long been taken to represent the invention of printing in the western world. In that role, it symbolizes one of the small handful of the greatest human accomplishments of all time. It can be considered along with such great ancient achievements as writing and numeration, along with such great modern achievements as the steam engine and the use of electricity.

Sometimes the importance of an invention—or of any human act—lies in what it leads to. It can truly be said that the invention of printing from movable metal type, in Germany in the middle of the fifteenth century, led to a radical change in the whole world of the intellect. It is this great invention that we are considering through the symbol of a single book, the Gutenberg Bible. Let us first take a look at the consequences of this invention from the perspectives of people living in Europe in the middle of the fifteenth century.

Books were available, but their text was of course written by hand. Today we sometimes think that all books are printed, and that texts written by hand should be called manuscripts. So they may: but the term "book" existed long before printing, and its meanings include any set of leaves, whether written or printed, that are bound together. Before printing, the making of a book was a laborious process, full of chances for error. It might take one scribe a full year to copy a single long book. Consequently books were very scarce and very expensive, and they were full of mistakes that the copyist had inevitably made in the course of his work.

Libraries existed in only a few centers of learning. In England at that time the abbey libraries at Canterbury and Bury were among the largest, with some 2,000 books each; but the Cambridge University Library had only 300, and very few learned men had any books at all. The most common books were Bibles, collections of psalms, and other books for religious services, almost entirely in Latin; after these, the most numerous books were writings from classical antiquity.

Although books were scarce, education was much more widespread in the later Middle Ages than is sometimes supposed. By 1450, in some areas of England for which there is evidence, up to thirty or forty percent of the adults were literate—that is, they could read. Writing was something separate, taught as an artisan skill, like shoemaking, with the rest of the literate world left to scribble as best it could. Hence our feeling, from looking at their handwriting, that great writers and notable personages of those times must have been partially illiterate and therefore probably stupid: such is our vanity that we can always turn to our own advantage a comparison between ourselves and talented people of the distant past.

There were many kinds of schooling available in England in the middle of the fifteenth century, and most children could get at least a rudimentary education, whatever their social or financial condition. Grammar schools (for the fortunate few) offered the best education, and the rich people had tutors for their children. But there was also a multitude of small and often informal parish schools taught by the clergy: the lesser clergy operated what were called chantry schools (associated with chapels for chanting masses), and even in tiny villages the priests or clerks taught the children of the parish. Learning was increasingly valued, and about this time the guilds of skilled artisans began to introduce minimum standards of education for membership. The Goldsmiths' Company, for example, passed a rule that no apprentice could be taken "without he can write and read."

The invention of printing provided books in abundance to serve the varieties of established schooling and to satisfy the hunger for learning. There was, in fact, a veritable explosion of books, an explosion heard around the western world. In the forty-five years after the Gutenberg Bible — by 1500, that is — more than ten million books had been printed, being copies of forty thousand different works. It would have taken all the copyists in Europe at least a thousand years to have turned out the books printed in those forty-five years. And that was only the merest beginning, the production of the years now called the incunable period, or the cradle of printing. When the invention outgrew its swaddling clothes, its effects really began to be felt. By 1500 there were 1,120 printing offices in 260 different towns in 17 European countries, and their output of printed books outran belief.

The result was a series of revolutions in learning. First, in the dissemination and increase of knowledge. Vastly more material became available for education in schools and for self-education. Earlier, teaching had been mainly oral; afterward, learning came mainly from reading. Those who were literate became very much more learned, and many achieved a depth of learning which only a few had ever before possessed. From this came an explosion of knowledge, the creation of new knowledge on a scale that had never before been imagined. Before then, the principal way of creating new knowledge had been through analysis of a limited number of authorities — primarily scripture and writings of classical antiquity. Free access to a greater body of knowledge was an important stimulant to creativity of other kinds, including experimental work. At the same time, the human intellect itself underwent a radical change in its adaptation to the demands of a very much greater body of knowledge and of new ways to deal with it, to use it, and to increase it.

The other revolution was a radical change in our social and political order as a result of a great increase in literacy. For a time, the literacy rate changed only rather slowly after the invention of printing. Education (of which literacy is a simple symptom) has generally had, at least from a large body of English-speaking peoples, a mixed reaction of awe and suspicion, as a state to be admired from a safe distance. Literacy gradually increased, however, because of the availability of the printed book and thanks to some legal nudges. Probably about thirty or forty percent of the adults in England were literate in the sixteenth and seventeenth centuries, approximately sixty percent in the eighteenth century, and perhaps ninety percent in our own time. The tremendous consequences of the increase in literacy were that it made democracy possible on more than a local level, and that it led to a social ordering on the bases of education and intellectual achievement, in addition to the earlier bases of wealth and family position. Thus it was that the invention of printing had a mighty influence, in crucial ways, on the development of the world as we know it today.

II

How DID THE invention of printing come to pass and how was the Gutenberg Bible produced? Most statements about the invention of printing are carefully limited to Europe and to movable type; these statements leave a considerable part of the globe unaccounted for and an indefinite number of other methods of printing unbespoken. Let me first indicate the reasons for these reservations.

The two historical methods of printing are block printing, and printing from movable type. In block printing, the outlines of words or pictures are carved on a block of wood, and an impression is made by inking the block and pressing a piece of paper (or vellum) on it. The disadvantages of block printing are numerous: the carving is very slow handwork, the outlines are relatively crude, the blocks wear out, and it is difficult to print from large blocks or from combinations of blocks. Printing from movable type involves placing individual letters or characters into lines (composing), adding lines until the desired page is full, and using a press to transfer ink to paper from a number of these pages at the same time. The advantages of printing from movable metal type were, at the outset, that it was fast, cheap, and clear; the type could be uniform, of any size desired, reusable, and capable of producing a relatively large number of impressions without wearing out.

Block printing existed before printing from movable type. The earliest dated European wood-block print is dated 1423; it is a picture, without words, of St. Christopher bearing the infant Christ. It is only a guess that wood-block printing was common in early times; all the extant European block books—blocks with text, that is—seem to be later than the Gutenberg Bible, and the method died in the sixteenth century.

The earliest printed book known is a ninth-century Chinese wood-block printing of the Diamond Sutra in the form of a roll sixteen feet long and one foot wide, made by pasting together the impressions from a lot of wood blocks. There was considerable block printing in China. Marco Polo, the wide-eyed traveler from Venice who visited China in the thirteenth century, tells of the marvelous Chinese printed money — black money on paper made from the bark of the mulberry tree, with the official seal on it in red ink. It was made by block printing, of course. Probably Marco Polo's wonder lay mostly in the opportunity that the ruler thus had to produce unlimited wealth for himself, a possibility we still have with us, still called "printing press money."

It was in China also that we first hear of printing from movable type, in the eleventh century. The type was made of pieces of clay, baked until it was hard, and the impression was taken by placing the paper on the type, apparently without the use of a press. (In Korea in the fifteenth century some type was made from copper and books were printed from it for a time.) The nature of the Chinese language inhibited the development of printing from movable type, however. Our basic alphabet has twenty-six characters, with constant repetition and hence both economy and manageability in reusing type. The Chinese language, with some forty thousand ideographs, was so ill-adapted to take advantage of movable type that printing never really developed in China in the early period. The Chinese experience had, in fact, no apparent influence whatsoever on the invention of printing in Europe.

The Chinese invention that was influential, however, was paper making. By the end of the first century of the Christian era, the Chinese had developed the making of paper, using treebark, hemp, rags, even old fish nets. The alleged inventor was Ts'ai Lun, a eunuch at the court of the emperor. Ts'ai Lun met his end in a striking manner: when he could not find his way out of a squabble between himself, the empress, and the emperor's grandmother, he went home, took a bath, combed his hair, put on his best clothes, and drank poison! His invention reached the Near East in the eighth century and came to Europe, through Spain, in the twelfth and thirteenth centuries.

The availability of inexpensive paper was crucial to the development of printing. The other requirements were a suitable metal alloy that could be used for type, and a machine that would cast uniform metal type speedily. With this preamble, the stage is set for the introduction of John Gutenberg, the invention of printing, and the Gutenberg Bible.

Our main sources of information on these subjects are twenty-eight legal documents which have been discovered in the course of the last five centuries. Several of them are lawsuits — unfortunately for Gutenberg, but fortunately for us, as even then lawsuits involved the recitation of background facts and the testimony of witnesses. Still, many matters about his life, about the invention of printing, and about the production of the book we call the Gutenberg Bible are far from clear, and there is room for dispute on large as well as small points. I will not explore those disputes but give a general account based on the primary documents and provide, for doubtful issues, the best scholarly consensus, so far as there is one. Learned men are no less contentious than the rest of the world, and small matters tend to rouse large passions.

John Gutenberg was born in the prosperous German city of Mainz, on the Rhine River, about the year 1399, or within the preceding five years. His family was formally classed, according to the ordering of the day, as "patrician," and they were prosperous, owning property and having income from annuities. Gutenberg was not content to live the usual life of a patrician, however. He seems to have been a restless man who probed into various new possibilities. He was something of a projector, bold and venturesome. He also had a strong will and a strong temper.

He early learned the craft of the goldsmith — though it was unusual for one in his social class to do so. When he was about twenty-nine, in 1428, Mainz was divided by a conflict between the artisans and the patricians. The artisans won, and Gutenberg had to go into exile; he went to Strasbourg, about a hundred and fifty miles up the Rhine.

There he moved in aristocratic circles and came to know a patrician woman named Ennelin zur Isernen Türe, and they planned to be married. Gutenberg apparently decided to back out, however, and the lady promptly brought suit against him for breach of promise. In the ecclesiastical court, a citizen named Claus Schott gave testimony against Gutenberg, which testimony (as the report went) "Gutenberg contradicted and rejected, declaring deponent to be a miserable wretch who lived by cheating and lying." For these utterances, Schott brought another suit against Gutenberg for the use of defamatory language, and he received provisional damages. How the breach of promise suit came out, we do not know; but eight years later the lady was still unmarried, and Gutenberg appears to have remained a bachelor for the rest of his life.

It was in Strasbourg that Gutenberg's restless mind started him on a career as an inventor and manufacturer. He developed a method for polishing precious stones. He worked out a way to manufacture mirrors, at a time when mirrors were uncommon and expensive. His experiments were doubtless costly, both in materials and in establishing a shop with skilled workmen. So he went into partnership with two other people, who contributed large sums of money in return for being taught what Gutenberg called his "secret arts." Their first plan was to make some special hand mirrors to sell to pilgrims going to Aachen (Aix-la-Chapelle) in 1439. When the pilgrimage was postponed for a year, the partners urged

Gutenberg to teach them his other "secret art," which seems to have been printing.

They hired a carpenter to build a press, based on the model of a wine press — a common item in this home of the glorious Rhine wines. They bought lead and other metals and began experimenting with casting type. The work was all done in great secrecy — on one occasion, the press was taken apart and the type melted down to avoid discovery. When one of the partners died, Gutenberg entered into litigation rather than let someone else learn the "secret arts." Harsh words were passed between the partners. Gutenberg's servant complained that a partner accused him of lying and that the partner also (in the words of the suit) "shouted to me publicly: 'Listen, soothsayer, you must tell the truth for me, even if I should get upon the gallows with you'; and thus he maliciously accused and charged me with being a perjured villain, whereby he did me injustice before the grace of God, which surely are very evil things."

Such partnerships do not seem destined to last forever, and this one expired legally in 1443. At about that time Gutenberg was able to return to Mainz — after an absence of some fifteen years. I do not know whether

PRINTING OFFICE, 1568. The two men in the background are setting type ("composing") by selecting the characters from the boxes ("the case") in front of them.

The two men in front are operating the printing press: the one on the left is removing a sheet of paper on which two pages have just been printed on one side; the one on the right is using circular pads ("balls") with handles to ink the type for two pages. In the foreground, on the left there is a stack of sheets that have already been printed, and on the right a stack of blank sheets of paper.

This illustration, as well as the three on the facing page, are wood engravings made from drawings by Jost Amman. They are reproduced from a book by Hartmann Schopper, printed in Frankfort in 1568. The methods here portrayed are thought to have been those followed, in general, for several hundred years after the invention of printing.

PAPERMAKER, 1568. The man is dipping a frame or mold of interwoven wires into a vat of smooth pulp. He will raise it from the vat and shake out the water; the wet sheet will then be removed from the mold, dried, and pressed. The boy is carrying a stack of finished sheets of paper. Parts of a water mill can be seen in the background; it was used in the process of washing, boiling, and beating linen rags until they became smooth pulp.

TYPEFOUNDER, 1568. The man is pouring molten metal into a mold to form the type. In front of him is a furnace with a fire inside and a bellows leaning against the wall. The metal (an alloy, with lead the main component) was melted on the top of the furnace. The face of the type was formed in a matrix which had been designed with a hard metal punch.

BOOKBINDER, 1568. The man in the background is sewing together folded sheets that have been printed. The man in the foreground is trimming, with a plane, the uneven edges of a set of sewn sheets. In front of him is a bound book in a hand press. Various tools of the bookbinder's trade are hanging on the wall above the shelf on which there are other books in process.

he was able to take the contents of his wine cellar with him or not; if so, it was quite a move, as, according to the tax record, it contained some 420 gallons. He continued his work on printing in Mainz for the next dozen years, until 1455, when the printing of the Gutenberg Bible was completed.

Being an inventor can be impoverishing, and being an entrepreneur may be bankrupting, particularly when almost all the financial entries are on the outgo pages and virtually none on the income ones. Gutenberg had very ambitious plans, and he exhausted his own funds in the first few years of his enterprising; thereafter he had to embark on the risky course of borrowing money which he hoped to repay from the uncertain returns of an indefinite future. He was carrying the interest (at 5%) on a loan that he had made in 1442 from the Parish of St. Thomas in Strasbourg; in 1448 he borrowed 150 guilders in Mainz, using a relative as security; in 1450 he had to borrow the very large sum of 800 guilders (at 6% interest) from a lawyer-capitalist-goldsmith named John Fust in order "to finish the work." But in two years, that money was gone, too, and he went back to Fust for another 800 guilders; this time the prudent Fust insisted on becoming a partner in the enterprise in order to protect his investment.

In the meantime, the experiments with printing were going forward. Several fonts of type were designed, a metal alloy was developed, a machine to cast type was invented, ink was worked out from the formula for oil paint introduced for painting some twenty years before by Jan van Eyck, and the press was perfected. About a dozen different works from this experimental period have been identified — often in fragmentary form as trash paper found in the binding of other books — and it is assumed that they were done by Gutenberg or his associates.

Perhaps the earliest one, printed between 1442 and 1454, is a tiny fragment of one leaf of a poem, in German, on the "World Judgment"; it is calculated, from this fragment, that the whole poem would have run to about seventy-four pages. There are fragments of various editions of a Latin grammar by Donatus. The earliest dated work (1454) is a Papal Indulgence, in several different issues; and there is a twelve-page leaflet, "A Warning to Christendom against the Turks" — timely in view of the fact that Constantinople had fallen the year before — concluding with the earliest printed New Year's greeting, for the year 1455: "Eyn gut selig nuwe Jar."

1455 proved to be a good but not a happy New Year for Gutenberg. It was a good year in that the printing of the Bible was finished. The text of the Bible is in Latin, in the version called the Vulgate, prepared by St. Jerome in the fourth century and in common use in the Roman Catholic Church. The version printed by Gutenberg was from a very accurate copy of the Paris revision, prepared by biblical scholars in the thirteenth century. Several passages of the Latin in the Gutenberg Bible are reproduced in this pamphlet, with the familiar English of the King James Version beside it. (The Vulgate is still sometimes thought of as the "Roman Catholic Bible"; when Harry S Truman took the oath of office as President of the United States in 1949, a peaceful balance was maintained by using two Bibles: a small English one for a Protestant Bible, and a facsimile of the Gutenberg Bible for a Catholic Bible.)

The beginning of the 23rd Psalm in the Latin of the Gutenberg Bible (below) and in the King James Version (the 1611 Bible) at the right. Notice the similarity of the two types. (The line above a vowel in the Latin is an abbreviation mark to indicate the omission of a following m or n.)

PSAL. XXIII.

Dauids confidence in Gods grace.

¶ A Psalme of Dauid.

HE LORD is * my shepheard, I shall not want.
2 He maketh me to lie downe in † greene pastures: he leadeth mee beside the † still waters.
3 He restoreth my soule: he leadeth me in the pathes of righteousnes, for his names sake.
4 Yea though I walke through the valley of the shadowe of death, * I will feare no euill: for thou art with me, thy

Luke 2:10-14 in the Gutenberg Bible (left) and in the 1611 Bible (right). (The copy of the 1611 Bible reproduced on these pages is the Bridgewater copy, with the Ellesmere crest on the cover.)

dixit illis angelus. Nolite timere. Ecce enim euangelizo uobis gaudium magnum qd erit omni populo: quia natus est uobis hodie saluator qui e cristus dns in ciuitate dauid. Et hoc uobis signum. Inuenietis infantem pannis inuolutum: et positum i presepio. Et subito facta est cum angelo multitudo militie celestis: laudantium deu et dicentium. Gloria i altissimis deo: et in terra pax hominibz bone uolutatis.

10 And the Angel said vnto them, Feare not : For behold, I bring you good tidings of great ioy, which shall be to all people.
11 For vnto you is borne this day, in the citie of Dauid, a Sauiour, which is Christ the Lord.
12 And this shall be a signe vnto you; yee shall find the babe wrapped in swadling clothes lying in a manger.
13 And suddenly there was with the Angel a multitude of the heauenly hoste praising God, and saying,
14 Glory to God in the highest, and on earth peace, good wil towards men.

The printing of the Gutenberg Bible was indeed a monumental task. It was set in type which had been designed to imitate handwriting. There were several different forms of handwriting in use by copyists; several examples of such handwriting — from famous manuscripts in the Huntington Library — are shown as illustrations in this pamphlet. These ex-

HANDWRITING AND EARLY TYPE. The passages on these two pages are samples from famous early manuscripts, in various forms of handwriting, for comparison with the type that was created for the Gutenberg Bible.

Below. From the Gutenberg Bible. The beginning of 1 Corinthians 13, as a basis for comparison.

At the bottom of this page. The same passage in the Gundulf Bible, a complete manuscript Bible in Latin written about the year 1080 as a memorial to Gundulf, Bishop of Rochester.

Facing page, top. A passage from William Langland's *Piers Plowman*, in an early 15th-century manuscript. This visionary poem is in alliterative Middle English verse. The passage reproduced starts with two Latin directions: "Here ends the fourth and last Passus of Do-better. Here begins the first Passus of Do-best."

Facing page, center. From Thomas Hoccleve's *Poems* in a manuscript book of about 1425 in the handwriting of the poet. Reproduced is the beginning of "La Male Regle": "O precious tresor incomparable/ O ground & roote of prosperitee." (This manuscript was once owned by the eldest son of King James I, Prince Henry, who died in 1612 when he was 18.)

Facing page, bottom. The Ellesmere Manuscript (about 1410) of Chaucer's *Canterbury Tales*, showing the beginning of the General Prologue: "Whan that Aprill with hise shoures soote/ The droghte of March hath perced to the roote/ And bathed every veyne in swich licour. . . ."

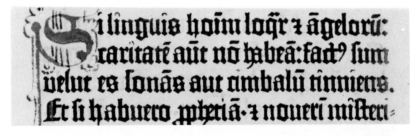

amples of handwriting can be compared with the printed text of the passages reproduced from the Gutenberg Bible. The specific form of handwriting which was the model for the type of this book was, naturally enough, the one in common use in Western Germany in the middle of the fifteenth century, called gothic. The type based on it is called gothic, or black letter.

The type of the Gutenberg Bible was designed and cast for this job, and the text was composed in two columns to the page and forty-two lines to

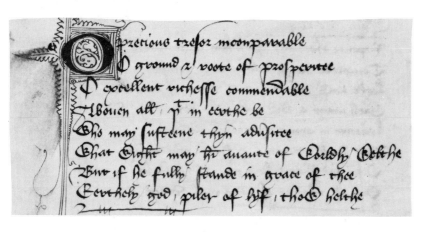

the column; hence it is sometimes called "the forty-two line Bible," though a few of the earlier pages set were in forty or forty-one lines. The complete Bible totals some 1,282 folio pages. At first, four compositors worked on it, then six; it is estimated that six compositors devoted two full years to typesetting alone. The printing began with one press, but soon six presses were in use; even so, it must have taken about two full years to see the sheets through the press. It is thought that something like one hundred and fifty copies were printed on paper, and thirty-five copies on vellum. It must have been a good year for Gutenberg.

The reason that 1455 was not a happy year for Gutenberg was that his financial house of cards fell down. The amount of capital needed to produce the Bible was enormous. There was the large cost of tools, equipment, wages, and of the experimental work during the preceding decade or more. Moreover, the paper and vellum for the Bible alone would have been a big investment; it is estimated that 5,000 calfskins were required for the thirty-five copies on vellum, and the equivalent of more than 50,000 sheets of paper 16½" x 12" for the one hundred and fifty copies on paper. (The paper would, in practice, have presumably been in the form of some 25,000 sheets twice the size of the leaves of the book, with two pages being printed on each side and the sheet folded once before binding; thus were two leaves, or a total of four printed pages, created in folio from each sheet of paper.) Of course all this material had to be bought and paid for a year or two before there was any possibility of a return from sales.

As a consequence, Gutenberg was not able to pay either the principal or the interest on his loans, and John Fust brought suit against him for an accumulated total debt of 2,026 guilders. Since Gutenberg had pledged his printing house equipment and supplies as security for the loan, Fust apparently took over the printing house and operated it himself in partnership with Peter Schoeffer, who seems to have been Gutenberg's foreman and who came to be related to Fust not only as a partner but (later) as son-in-law. It is presumed that the partnership of Fust and Schoeffer commenced before the printing of the Bible was quite complete. In any event, they went on later to produce other estimable books, most notably a beautiful Psalter of 1457, and another Bible in 1462.

The career of Gutenberg after the termination of his partnership with Fust is somewhat obscure. He may have been allowed to retain part of the earlier printing equipment, and it is sometimes argued that he continued a career as a printer in Mainz and Bamberg, perhaps producing an encyclopedia called the *Catholicon* and a thirty-six line Bible. He was given a pension by the Archbishop of Mainz in 1465, and he died in obscurity in 1468, at the age of about sixty-nine.

But Gutenberg was not without honor in his own time. Among the many contemporary references to him as the inventor of printing, perhaps none is more rewarding than a letter by the Rector of the University of Paris, Professor Guillaume Fichet, written on December 31, 1470, and printed in 1471, just a couple of years after Gutenberg's death and only some fifteen years after the Bible was printed. (The fact that Fichet was writing in Latin may have loosed him from inhibitions and encouraged a freedom with superlatives, a freedom to be found in the Latin compositions of many Renaissance writers.) "Not far from the city of Mainz" he wrote, "there appeared a certain John whose surname was Gutenberg, who, first of all men, devised the art of printing, whereby books are made, not by a reed, as did the ancients, nor with a quill pen, as do we, but with metal letters, and that swiftly, neatly, beautifully. Surely this man is worthy to be loaded with divine honors by all the Muses, all the arts, all the tongues of those who delight in books, and is all the more to be preferred to gods and goddesses in that he has put the means of choice within reach of letters themselves and of mortals devoted to culture. That great Gutenberg has discovered things far more pleasing and more divine, in carving out letters in such fashion that whatever can be said or thought can by them be written down at once and transcribed and committed to the memory of posterity." The praise is deserved, and these comments can still stand as an epitome of the contribution of the invention of printing to the progress of learning.

III

THE SURVIVAL RATE of copies of the Gutenberg Bible has been high. Today, more than five hundred years after publication, forty-seven copies are recorded: of these, thirty-five are printed on paper and twelve on vellum. If the estimate is correct that the total number originally printed was one hundred and eighty-five copies (one hundred and fifty on paper, thirty-five on vellum), the overall survival rate is about one in four, or one in three for those on vellum. (There are, in addition, some fragments and separate leaves which are not usually counted as copies.)

Some of these forty-seven copies are not complete, however. Substantial parts are lacking in thirteen of them (two on vellum and eleven on paper), thus leaving thirty-four copies that can be called complete (with no more than a few leaves, in one case fourteen, which are missing). Since two of the complete copies (recorded as belonging to libraries in Germany) have not been seen since World War II, there may in fact be no more than thirty-two complete copies in existence.

But to return to forty-seven, the total of the complete copies, the incomplete copies, and the missing copies. These are distributed around the world: fourteen are in the United States, eleven in Germany, eight in Great Britain, four in France, two each in Spain and Italy, one each in Portugal, Switzerland, Austria, Denmark, Belgium, and Poland.

Of the fourteen copies in the United States, three are on vellum (all of them complete), one at the Library of Congress, one at the Pierpont Morgan Library, and one at the Huntington; of the eleven copies on paper, eight are complete and three are incomplete. The Huntington copy is the only copy considered complete, on either vellum or paper, which is not on the east coast. (Our copy actually lacks two leaves, the last one in each volume, which were supplied in facsimile before 1825.) The first copy to come to this country was bought for $2,600 at auction in London on March 13, 1847, for James Lenox of New York; this copy, on paper, is now in the New York Public Library.

Copies do move around occasionally, though it would take both a great deal of patience and money to get a copy. Since the Huntington copy was acquired in 1911, about fourteen copies have changed hands; all but two or three have found their way into institutional libraries, either by gift or purchase, and presumably the other private copies are in due course destined for institutional ownership. Many copies have been in libraries for centuries; the University of Leipzig, for example, has had its copy since at least 1543. Originally, most of the copies were housed, presumably, in the libraries of monasteries, churches, and ecclesiastical bodies. A copy now in the Bibliothèque Nationale in Paris belonged, as early as 1457, to the church in Ostheim; it is also distinguished by being inscribed with the earliest date that appears on any copy — 24 August 1456 on the first volume and 15 August 1456 on the second volume, the dates on which the rubricator (Henricus Cremer) completed his work.

The Huntington copy, which includes both the Old and the New Testaments, is one of the twelve copies on vellum (and one of the ten complete vellum copies) that are known to exist. It is imposing in physical appearance: it is bound in two massive volumes; together, they weigh fifty-three and a quarter pounds, suitable for the weightiness of the contents. Ours is one of nine copies recorded as being in fifteenth-century bindings. The wooden boards in the binding of our copy are thought to be part of the original, uniform binding of the two volumes done between 1455 and 1460, though the pigskin covering the boards was renewed in the early sixteenth century. The covers are stamped with a design, and early thumb index tabs (in faded red) are attached to leaves beginning the several books of the Bible to indicate their location. Somewhat later, metal clasps were added to keep each volume closed, and metal bosses were attached to the outside of the covers to protect them from wear and damage.

Both volumes are kept on public exhibition in the tower case specially made to display them. The pages are turned several times a year to reduce the hazard of fading.

The leaves of our copy are exceedingly bright. The vellum has hardly darkened, even with the passage of more than five centuries, and the ink used for the text is still glossy black.

The gothic (or black letter) type is clear, and as legible as such type can be for those who did not early in life come to terms with German script. Several variations of gothic type soon developed, and within the first half century of printing the two other major families of early type — roman and italic — were created. The sample passages reproduced on these pages

The following passages from early printed books of distinction can give some idea of the range of types developed within the fifteenth century.

From the Gutenberg Bible. The beginning of I Corinthians 13, as a basis for comparison with the types in the passages which follow.

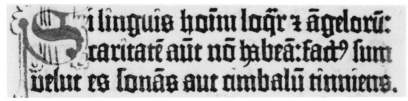

From a Bible printed in Latin in 1462 by Fust and Schoeffer. The conclusion of the colophon at the end of the book, followed by the first use of a printer's device.

From William Caxton's *Recuyell of the Historyes of Troye*, 1475. Caxton's explanation that his book is printed and not written. (This is the first book printed in English; this copy is said to have belonged to the Queen Elizabeth who was the wife of King Edward IV.)

From Pliny's *Natural History*, printed in Latin by Nicholas Jenson in 1472 in Venice. From Book 17, chapter 2, concerning the effect of location and weather on trees. (An early use of roman type, in contrast to the gothic or black-letter types of the passages above; this type can also be compared with the handwriting of the Gundulf Bible, shown on page 12.)

show how the type of the Gutenberg Bible compares with the type of several other famous books that came after it.

When the Gutenberg Bible had been printed, the sheets were handed over (much as was the case with manuscripts) to specialists who added the art work by hand. The rubricator did the pen ornamentation in colored ink (particularly red and blue), the illuminator added the gold work, and either the illuminator or another artist did the paintings in the margins and in the initial letters. The decorations shine with such rich colors that one can hardly believe they were applied immediately after the book was printed and have never since been touched up. The predominant colors are red, blue, and gold. The page headings, the chapter numbers, the chapter initials, and the large initials are in color.

At the beginning of each of the books of the Bible, there is usually an elaborate decoration in color in a margin, with leaves, sprays, birds, animals, and illustrative drawings. Sometimes a margin is full of drawings, as is the inner margin of the first page of the Book of Genesis, which is shown on page 37: God is at the top, in the act of creation; in the panel below are some of the works of creation, the fish of the sea on the fifth day and the beasts of the earth on the sixth day, with the creation of Eve out of Adam as the last act shown. This reproduction deserves, and will repay, careful scrutiny of its details and of its total effect. It is only about one quarter the size of the original, but even so it gives a reasonable idea of this magnificent book. The leaves of the Huntington copy measure about 16¼″ tall and 12″ wide; it is one of four (the others being in Rome, Tübingen, and Leipzig) that are the largest of all known copies.

Most of the books of the Bible have a small drawing in the large initial

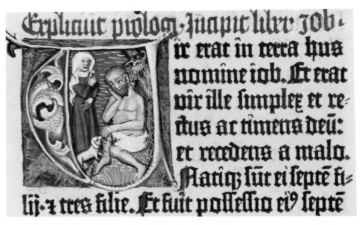

Beginning of the Book of Job. "Vir erat in terra hus nomine iob . . ." (There was a man in the land of Uz, whose name was Job; and that man was perfect and upright, and one that feared God, and eschewed evil.)

letter with which the book commences. Job is portrayed with a dog licking his sores, Daniel with toothy lions on either side of him, and the Psalms begin with a picture of King David playing on his harp.

Beginning of the Book of Daniel. "Anno tercio regni ioachim regis iuda venit . . ." (In the third year of the reign of Jehoiakim king of Judah came Nebuchadnezzar king of Babylon unto Jerusalem, and besieged it.)

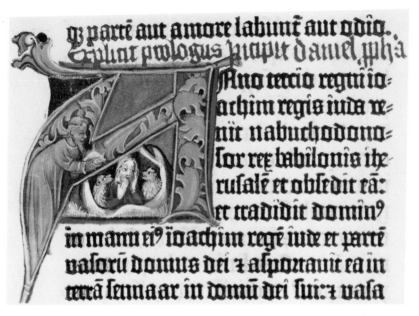

Beginning of the Book of Psalms. "Beatus vir qui non abiit in consilio impiorum . . ." (Blessed is the man that walketh not in the counsel of the ungodly, nor standeth in the way of sinners, nor sitteth in the seat of the scornful.)

There are many notable decorations in the Huntington copy of the Gutenberg Bible. There is, for example, a hunting scene in which two dogs are chasing their prey all across one lower margin. In the bottom margin of the Book of Proverbs, a peacock has his magnificent tail spread into the shape of a full fan, while a nearby insect — a bee, perhaps —

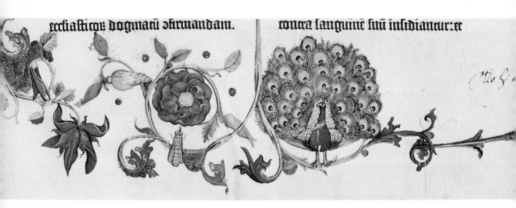

edges toward an open flower. In the left margin beside the Song of Solomon, five different kinds of birds are posed for their portraits on a gracefully stylized branch which has four varieties of flowers.

The decorations throughout both volumes are splendid examples of medieval art.

IV

The Huntington copy of the Gutenberg Bible was acquired in 1911, in a dramatic way and with fascinating consequences.

This copy had been the property of an important New York collector, Robert Hoe. He had bought it in 1898, in great secrecy, from a London dealer, Bernard Quaritch. Hoe sent a handwritten letter (which is in our collection) to Quaritch offering to buy it; he was very apologetic, however, because he already owned a copy on paper. "It seems absurd," he wrote, "for me to have two copies of so expensive a book, but I would like to own the Vellum Copy." (This is the true collector's instinct in action.) "Is there any way," he said, "of getting it here without *any one* knowing I had it?" Nobody: not even the Quaritch employees. There was, and he got it, for $25,000.

This book was the chief item in the Hoe Sale, which took place in the Anderson Galleries in New York, in April 1911, after the death of Robert Hoe. The sale catalog tempted all collectors with the following words, in full capitals: "IT IS THEREFORE PROBABLE THAT NO OTHER OPPORTUNITY WILL WILL EVER OCCUR TO OBTAIN A VELLUM COPY OF THIS MONUMENTAL WORK, THE FIRST IMPORTANT BOOK PRINTED FROM MOVABLE TYPE."

On Monday evening, April 24, the sales room was crowded with dealers and collectors. The most notable European dealers were present, including the Bernard Quaritch whose father had sold the Bible to Hoe. The auctioneer, Sidney Hodgson, was brought from London to handle the sale. Joseph Widener, a wealthy collector from Philadelphia, was sitting in the middle of the front row; the firm of Dodd & Livingston was ready for heavy action; and George D. Smith, the dealer who was to bid for Henry E. Huntington, was in place with Huntington at his side.

The crowd was tense with excitement, and applause rippled through the room when the Gutenberg Bible was announced by the auctioneer in his clipped British accent. He asked for an opening bid, and a wag in the back of the room said, "A hundred dollars." Nervous laughter. Dodd & Livingston started the auction at $10,000, and the bidding moved quickly to $31,000, where that firm dropped out. Quaritch's last bid was $33,000. Only Widener and Smith were left. At $41,000, they began to move by five hundreds, and then by two hundreds. Then Smith increased the pace and said "$46,000." "$47,000," replied Widener. "$48,000," countered Smith. There was a perceptible pause, and then Widener said "$49,000." "$50,000," immediately replied Smith, and there was no answer. The auctioneer raised his hammer, held it a moment, and then let it fall. The audience broke into spontaneous applause, so prolonged that A. Edward Newton (a collector who was present) later wrote of it as one of the great moments he had experienced in the auction rooms.

"Let's see the purchaser! Let him stand up," someone shouted, Smith stood up, Widener slipped out of the room almost unobserved, and it was announced that Huntington was the purchaser. Many of those present felt that they were witnessing an epochal event: the highest price ever given for any book ever sold at auction, the unbelievable sum of $50,000, and the national pride of having the event take place in New York with an American as the purchaser.

Not everyone was pleased, however. Some of the European dealers were disgruntled at their lack of success in the sale, and J. P. Morgan's librarian, Miss Belle da Costa Greene, "left the auction room in a huff," according to the newspapers. The prices, she declared, "are perfectly ridiculous. They are more than ridiculous — they are most harmful. They establish a dangerous precedent." "The Hoe collection is being sold practically en bloc," she said, to the same man who bought the Gutenberg Bible. "It has hardly been an auction at all," she fumed. "Buyers have come from all over Europe and are getting nothing."

The great news of the sale of the Gutenberg Bible was carried in hundreds of newspapers throughout the United States, from Burlington, Vermont to Phoenix, Arizona, from Birmingham, Alabama to Muncie, Indiana to Denver, Colorado. The typical story ran about six inches and began with an awed declaration of the price; it told a little about the book, a little about Huntington, and made some mention of other early books of interest. It is hard to imagine any bookish event that would today command that kind of attention in what are now styled the public media.

It is even harder to imagine the kind of attention that the sale gained on the editorial pages. It is astonishing that there were, in the course of a couple weeks after the sale, just about as many editorials as there had been news stories, and the editorials tended to be longer. There seem to have been more moralists than book collectors among those editorial writers. Almost all of them dwelt on the price, and there was about an equal distribution of sweet and sour in their opinions. One declared, with more hope than logic, that "When Bibles sell for $50,000 it can't be said that Christianity is on the wane." The Louisville *Courier-Journal* sourly asserted that the sum was paid simply "for the gratification of vanity. . . . From the Gutenberg Bible Mr. Huntington can derive not a whit more artistic, literary or spiritual pleasure than he could get from a 50-cent edition or even from a free copy which any kindly-disposed Christian would cheerfully give him."

The San Francisco *Star* condemned the purchase as an anti-humanitarian act, saying that "one empty stomach is of more moment to humanity than many Gutenberg Bibles," but the Chico, California *Enterprise* found a ray of hope, saying that "Henry E. Huntington will squeeze half way through the needle's eye if the Lord will let him. The day after he paid $50,000 for the Gutenberg Bible he donated $25,000 to the half million dollar Y.M.C.A. fund."

Huntington's clipping service dutifully supplied him with this vast quantity of clippings, which we still have. We also still have the avalanche of personal letters that descended on him, and to read them (as I have done) is to become aware of the fact that there are many people out there who have pen in hand, eager to write. In this case, everybody had something to sell. I hope that the flavor will come through from one or two brief examples. From the Comfort Sanitary Poultry Farm — "Texas' Largest Baby-chick Hatchery" — in Comfort, Kendall County, Texas, this short classic: "I read in the paper that you are the buyer of that Gutenberg bible and having in possession an old Bible myself I am asking the favor from you to let me know how I can find out what my bible is worth. It might be I will sell it. The book was printed in 1747 and is bound in hog skin." (It ought to last.) Bibles without number were offered, some having belonged to a grandfather, all "very valuable." He was offered sundry other books, including *Pilgrim's Progress* in Welsh, six French books printed in 1812, an 1822 volume on dentistry, the 1816 memoirs of James Wilkinson, a Confederate bond, the writings of Josephus, the sermons of John Boys, and a copy of Cowper's poems sent from England with 32 cents postage due. He was also offered a harpsichord, an old leather head rest, a gentleman's inlaid shaving mirror, a pair of antlers "beautifully mounted," an Old English thermometer — once the property of Beowulf, perhaps — a silver watch with Columbus' ships painted on the face, and about a thousand other objects of vertu.

One letter, from Alexander, Kansas, was addressed to Huntington "c/o the late Collis P. Huntington, New York City, New York." Collis had been dead for eleven years, but the letter was delivered—though not, I believe, by the routing called for in the address.

Another letter came direct from Tucson, Arizona, from a friend named Epes Randolph. "Dear Mr. Huntington: I have known for many years that you were sadly in need of the influence imparted by a constant use of Holy Writ, but I did not suppose that on short notice you would feel the need of $50,000 worth of it 'in a bunch.' "

Huntington replied, "My dear Randolph: I certainly should not have paid $50,000 for that Bible if I had not needed it very much, although, as a matter of fact, I found after I had purchased it that I could buy one for 10 cents, the contents of which would probably have done me as much good as the one I have, so you can imagine how chagrined I felt that I had paid $50,000 for one."

In fact, he was not chagrined at all. The Gutenberg Bible gave him intense pleasure, and he delighted in looking at it, in thinking about what it stands for, and in showing it to his guests. It continues to be a delight to visitors, and it is perhaps a greater attraction than is any other single book in the Library.

It is truly a monumental work, a landmark in learning. It deserves our attention and our respect as a worthy symbol of a revolution in our intellectual life.

William Shakespeare
at the Huntington

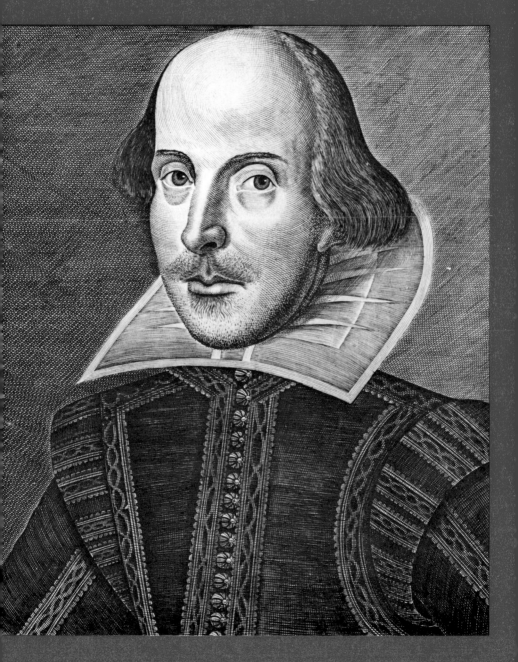

or there is nothing
either good or bad, but thinking makes it fo

here's a Diuinity that fhapes our ends,
Rough-hew them how we will.

here's Rofemary,
thats for remembrance,
pray you loue re-
member, and there is Pancies,
thats for thoughts.

here is fpeciall prouidence,in
the fall of a Sparrowe, if it be, tis not to come , if it be not to come,
it will be now, if it be not now, yet it well come , the readines is all

About the illustrations

Over. The portrait of William Shakespeare is from the engraving, by Martin Droeshout, which appeared as the frontispiece to the earliest published collection of Shakespeare's plays (known as the First Folio, 1623). Only two portraits are generally considered as authentic likenesses, this one and the bust in the Stratford Church.

Facing page. The Shakespeare Garden at the Huntington, viewed from over the shoulder of the bust of Shakespeare.

Decorative initials and borders are all from the First Folio.

Facsimile quotations are all from *Hamlet;* the First Quarto (1603), the Second Quarto (1604), and the First Folio (1623) are represented.

62

WILLIAM SHAKESPEARE was a very wise Englishman. Like other wise Englishmen, he would probably have availed himself of the chance to visit the Huntington, if he could have done so. And, like them, he would undoubtedly have come in the winter time. Unhappily, our times are out of joint.

But William Shakespeare is at the Huntington now, anyway, in various real ways. In the garden named for him. In the many books that we have published about him. Most of all, perhaps, in the work of scholars using our collection of the earliest editions of his plays and poems—a collection which has sometimes been described as the best in the world.

These rare and unusual books are necessary in working on some of the many problems that face Shakespeare scholars, and I will describe one or two of those problems. That will lead us to what lay behind the publication of these books, and to something of Shakespeare's professional career. Some ingenious people have found quick ways of knowing about Shakespeare by creating their own evidence, and I will touch on their work. Finally, I would like to offer a glimpse into the world of book collecting through the story of how the Shakespeare rarities came to be assembled here. I begin, however, with a problem.

I

When we first meet Hamlet in the opening act of the play, he is in what might now be called, rather solemnly, a parent-child confrontation with his mother and his new stepfather. They want him to change his ways: to be more cheerful, to stop mourning his dead father, to give up the university, and to live at home. Today he might say that they were hassling him. Most any son at any time would claim that he was being pushed around.

Hamlet is, by turns, surly, cryptic, verbose, and resigned. As soon as he is alone for the first time, we realize that he is suffering from a deep emotional upset. In his rambling, illogical, melodramatic, first soliloquy, he tells us that he is thinking of suicide. Here is the beginning of the passage in the form we usually know it:

> O that this too too solid flesh would melt,
> Thaw, and resolve itself into a dew!
> Or that the Everlasting had not fix'd
> His canon 'gainst self-slaughter! O God! God!
> How weary, stale, flat, and unprofitable
> Seem to me all the uses of this world!

The words of this soliloquy were actually very different in the first printing of the play, in 1603, in what is called the First Quarto. There Hamlet says:

Ham. O that this too much griev'd and fallied flesh
Would melt to nothing, or that the vniuerfall
Globe of heauen would turne al to a Chaos!

In the Second Quarto, of 1604, the words are nearer the familiar language; but instead of regretting the law against "self-slaughter," he laments "seale slaughter" and instead of being "weary" of the uses of the world, he is "wary" of them.

> *Ham.* O that this too too fallied flesh would melt,
> Thaw and refolue it felfe into a dewe,
> Or that the euerlasting had not fixt
> His cannon gainst feale flaughter, ô God, God,
> How wary, stale, flat, and vnprofitable
> Seeme to me all the vfes of this world?

For the whole length of the play, wide divergences in language are found in the earliest printings of *Hamlet*. The best-known passage in the play, or perhaps in any of the plays, is Hamlet's deep meditation on death, when Polonius and Claudius are getting ready to spy on him. He says, as we usually remember it:

> To be, or not to be—that is the question:
> Whether 'tis nobler in the mind to suffer
> The slings and arrows of outrageous fortune,
> Or to take arms against a sea of troubles,
> And by opposing end them.

However, the First Quarto has Hamlet speaking very different words:

> *Ham.* To be, or not to be, I there's the point,
> To Die, to fleepe, is that all? I all:
> No, to fleepe, to dreame, I mary there it goes,
> For in that dreame of death, when wee awake,
> And borne before an euerlasting Iudge,
> From whence no passenger euer retur'nd,

Probably these words jangle in your ears, but what is most important is to try to determine whether they are what Shakespeare intended for us. Shakespeare is, I believe, the greatest writer in English. If we are reading him, our ambition should be to read what he wrote.

One basic form of scholarship, called textual criticism, concerns itself with trying to determine the words that the writer intended for us. Did Shakespeare write, "To be, or not to be—that is the question"? Or did he write, "To be, or not to be, I here's the point"? A single passage may not matter much, but you can multiply the question a thousand times in *Hamlet* alone.

When Hamlet dies, are his last words "Farewel *Horatio*, heauen receiue my soule" (Q1)? Or are they "the rest is silence," with

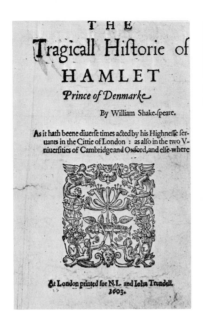

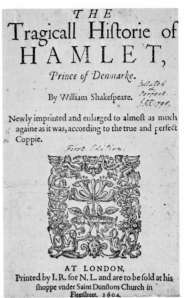

Horatio replying ". . . good night sweete Prince, / And flights of Angels sing thee to thy rest" (Q2)? When Ophelia is being buried, does Hamlet's mother say "I thought thy bride-bed to have deckt sweet maide, / And not haue strew'd thy graue" (Q2)? Or was her thought "to adorne thy bridale bed, faire maide, / And not to follow thee vnto thy graue" (Q1)?

The questions can be repeated almost endlessly for every Shakespeare play for which there is more than one early edition with any authority, and the ultimate difference is between the plays as written or rewritten by Shakespeare and the plays as remembered by actors, mistaken by printers, and corrupted by editors. For these passages from *Hamlet*, I have been quoting from the First Quarto (Q1), and from the Second Quarto (Q2), and from the first collection of his plays, called the First Folio, of 1623 (F1). It turns out that all of them are crucial to deciding what Shakespeare actually wrote, and the Huntington Library is the only place in the world that has all of these original texts.

Getting the text right is always one of the basic forms of scholarship. The problems with Shakespeare are very severe and very important. The First Quarto of *Hamlet* of 1603 was, perhaps, reconstructed by several actors who wrote down the parts as they remembered them (not too well), a process today called "memorial reconstruction"; this kind of quarto is known as a "Bad Quarto"—

not for moral reasons, but because memory played many tricks with the text. It is also argued that this quarto is not a memorial reconstruction but rather a deliberate abridgement made by the acting company for performances on tour in the provinces. No one can be absolutely sure which it is. In any event, the publisher obtained the copy for the book illegally, though the book was printed very carefully. The Second Quarto, of 1604, is thought to have been based on Shakespeare's own manuscript—known in the trade as his "foul papers"—from which the acting company's script was made, but the printing was very sloppy and full of errors. The Folio of 1623 was apparently based, for this play, on the acting company's official prompt book which included later revisions, probably by the author, and it was printed accurately; but it was by then some twenty-two years after their first production of the play, and the company usually considered plays over ten years old as much in need of revision or refurbishing to attract an audience. All three versions are different in hundreds of ways: each may contain some Shakespeare that the others don't have, and perhaps a lot of not-Shakespeare too. The problem is to take them all and establish a single, consistent version that would be the closest thing to what Shakespeare would have wanted us to have.

You might think that the easiest solution to the problem would be simply to take whichever words seem to make best sense, and this was in fact the usual method of textual criticism before this century. But who knows what is "best sense"? The trouble is that every age would remake Shakespeare according to its own taste, and what we should want is Shakespeare's sense.

The most authoritative solution would then seem to be to compare the different editions with Shakespeare's own manuscript. Alas, there are no extant Shakespeare manuscripts of any of his plays or his poems. Moreover, Shakespeare took no hand in the printing of any of his plays, and (so far as we know) he did not even retain a manuscript of any one of them. This is not to say that he didn't care about his plays, or that he was indifferent to them—only that he did not, within the pattern of his times, involve himself in their perpetuation in reading form. Hence the earliest printed editions of *Hamlet* and the other plays (and poems) remain the fundamental sources of our knowledge of Shakespeare.

67

A CATALOGVE

of the feuerall Comedies, Hiſtories, and Tragedies contained in this Volume.

The table of contents of the First Folio (1623).

II

To set this problem about Shakespeare in its context—and many other Shakespeare problems as well, including why there are no manuscripts—it is worth going into the role of the playwright in Shakespeare's time, and into matters of his life and his professional career.

For Shakespeare was, most of all, a professional man of the theater, someone who was as deep in the show business of his time as it was possible to be. He would be, in modern terms, a combination of a very prominent actor, an eminent producer, a leading businessman in the film industry, the best writer of the time, and more. Shakespeare came down to London from Stratford in the 1580s, a young man in his twenties, from a substantial middle-class family, with a locally-prominent ambitious father and a mother from the landed gentry, the oldest of six children, with a good grammar school education, and an early marriage and three children of his own. In saying these things, I am not trying to account for or explain genius— no one can do that—but rather to reassure us all of Shakespeare's reality, of his rootedness in the actual world.

In London, a city of about 150,000 people and the only sizeable one in England at the time, Shakespeare began as an actor, soon wrote plays himself, and became one of the founding members of the Lord Chamberlain's Men—later chosen to be the King's Men—the best of the two or three acting companies in London. Their other notable actors were Richard Burbage (for whom such roles as Hamlet, Othello, and Lear were written), and Will Kempe (the chief comic), though the rest of the company took turns in performing the

Below: This view of London, showing the Thames and the neighborhood of the Globe Theatre, is from Merian's view of 1638 in an engraving by Pierre d'Avity, Frankfurt, 1646

best parts. The company had about fifteen members, of whom a dozen were men and three or four were boys whose voices had not yet changed and who played all the female parts.

I suppose that most readers of Shakespeare have been puzzled by the fact that there are relatively few female parts in the plays: generally only two to four women are named, while there are ten to thirty men. The explanation is not that Shakespeare disliked women — he was too wise for that, surely — but rather that the number of boys in the company was small. Likewise, readers may notice that there are many fewer mothers than fathers in Shakespeare, and that almost no mother-child relationships are presented sympathetically. Instead of guessing that Shakespeare hated his mother, however, we might better assume that the role of a mature, loving mother was beyond the powers of the boy actors.

The company, as a group, was owned by half a dozen of its members, who acted as partners in operating it and sharing the profits. Shakespeare was one of the partners. The company put on about 250 performances a year, in repertory, principally by rotating their newer plays. Three performances in the first month was about the limit for a new play, and after a dozen performances — over a period of a year or more — the play was put on less often. The company might perform thirty different plays in the course of a year, and nearly half of them would have to be new plays. So they were constantly in need of new material, much as is the case with today's television. And there were no shows comparable to "I Love Lucy," which could be rerun seventeen or seventy times, nor was there an audience of children who would look at anything rather than go to bed. There was much work for writers, in writing plays and in refurbishing old ones, in filling the hungry mouth of the theater.

As a part owner, Shakespeare wrote plays for the company; indeed, all of his plays were written for the company. In his long career of more than twenty years in the theater, he averaged almost two plays a year: a total of thirty-seven plays, in the usual reckoning, plus portions of several others. In writing for the company, Shakespeare made parts for all of the members. Today, we often have plays with only half a dozen parts, or even as few as two or three. No Shakespeare play has a cast of less than fifteen, and some have forty or fifty parts, but so arranged that the company of fifteen could handle them all by doubling.

When Shakespeare finished writing a play, he considered that the manuscript belonged to his company rather than to him personally, and it was for them to deal with the manuscript as they saw fit. They turned it into a handwritten script, called the book of the play, or the prompt book, and it became a valuable part of the company's possessions.

Romeo and Juliet *quartos.*
Four rare early editions.

It was distinctly to their disadvantage for a current play to be printed and so made available for some touring company to perform. When a play from the active repertory found its way into print —and this happened about half the time, at least in Shakespeare's case—there was a fuss and an outcry, and often a later edition was put out, perhaps at Shakespeare's behest, to replace the "stolen and surreptitious copy" which so imperfectly represented his work.

These slender editions of individual plays—called "quartos" because four leaves were created by twice folding the big sheets they were printed on—these editions were issued by London printers and booksellers as paperbacks, about 64 to 128 pages in length. The Huntington copies of these plays are all now bound in the finest leather, levant morocco, in very elegant bindings individually designed by T. J. Cobden-Sanderson or Macdonald or Bedford or Rivière or some other notable artist-craftsman of the late nineteenth century. These thin volumes, bound in a great variety of tasteful colors—green, crimson, cream, red, blue, maroon, purple—are gracious to the hand and to the eye, and they reflect the rarity and cost of the work they house. Sometimes the original book has been taken apart and each of its leaves mounted in a larger sheet to give the book even greater presence and importance. Very few copies come on the market these days. In the last decade, only a couple have been available, at about $10,000 each, and they of less desirable editions. A desirable edition might command a price in the range of $50,000-$100,000.

Originally, as I said, these quartos were sold as very simple paperbacks, at a price of about six pence. That was about the cost of a simple, plain meal in a London tavern; or, to convert it to modern

71

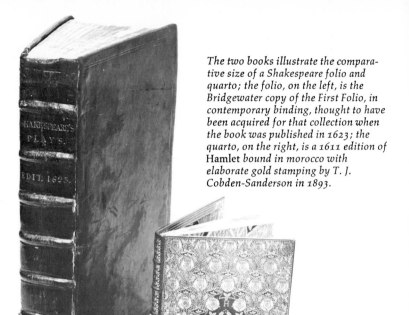

*The two books illustrate the compara-
tive size of a Shakespeare folio and
quarto; the folio, on the left, is the
Bridgewater copy of the First Folio, in
contemporary binding, thought to have
been acquired for that collection when
the book was published in 1623; the
quarto, on the right, is a 1611 edition of*
Hamlet *bound in morocco with
elaborate gold stamping by T. J.
Cobden-Sanderson in 1893.*

values, the cost of eating out at a fast-food establishment. The number of copies printed for each quarto was probably about 1,000. These paperbacks were ephemeral in nature: few bookish people or serious collectors bothered to keep them, because current plays ranked very low in their system of literary value. A sonnet might be thought to confer immortality on its subject—as Shakespeare repeatedly said it would—but no such claim was made for a play. In any event, these play quartos quickly disappeared, being read out of existence, passed around, thrown away. Hence their great rarity today and the relatively few extant copies that have been recorded after centuries of search. For example, the median number of recorded copies of the quarto editions of Shakespeare's plays that were published before his death in 1616 is about six. Eighteen of his plays (from among the thirty-seven now commonly regarded as the body of his work) had been published in quarto before he died, some in more than one edition; in fact, something like forty-six different editions (including variants, depending on how you count them) before 1616 are recorded, and the Huntington Library has one or more copies of thirty-seven of those forty-six. Between the time of his death and the publication of the First Folio, in 1623, thirteen more quarto editions were published (including one play that had not before been printed), and I am happy to say that the Huntington has all thirteen of them.

So Shakespeare was an actor, and a partner in an acting company, and a writer. These do not exhaust his professional activities, however, as he was also a part owner of a theater, the famous Globe, on the south bank of the river Thames. He and several of his partners in the acting company banded together and, in a separate venture, had it built in 1599. This was the theater for which Shakespeare wrote his greatest plays. Since it is the most renowned theater in our tradition, it is perhaps worth reiterating how it differed—so far as we know the details—from theaters of our personal experience.

It was large, accommodating perhaps 2,500 people, or roughly the size of the Ahmanson Theater in the Los Angeles Music Center, or the Pasadena Civic Auditorium. But it was very different in style and method of presentation. The Globe was circular in form, the walls vertical, and there were three levels of covered galleries within the perimeter. The center was open to the sky, and the stage was a high rectangular platform jutting halfway across the open courtyard, with the back part of it roofed, behind a pair of pillars. There were no seats in the courtyard, and people paid one penny—the price of a bottle of ale, say—to stand there, on any of the three sides of the large platform stage, which was about forty feet wide and thirty feet deep. It cost an extra penny to be in the galleries, which had seats. Wherever you sat or stood, you were relatively near the action on the big platform stage, and the audience doubtless had a much greater sense of participation than one has today in an old-fashioned theater with the stage behind an arch and a curtain. In the Globe, very little scenery was used, or props, and the language of the play set the scene. There were no intermissions as we know them—when the members of the audience leave their seats and go out to smoke or drink—but the act-structure is still not clearly understood; within the acts the performance was continuous except for occasional short pauses like those between movements in a symphony.

The Globe was a very successful venture, but it burned down shortly after Shakespeare retired to Stratford. The company was putting on, in 1613, a play that called for much pomp and pageantry, *Henry VIII*, probably written by Shakespeare in collaboration with Fletcher. In the course of the play, they shot off a cannon, and no one noticed that the wadding landed on the thatched roof over the galleries. In an hour's time, the whole place was in ashes. Miraculously, everyone survived. One observer, Sir Henry Wotton, light-heartedly reported that "nothing did perish, but wood and straw, and a few forsaken cloaks; only one man had his breeches set on fire, that would perhaps have broyled him, if he had not by the benefit of a provident wit put it out with bottle Ale." The owners busied themselves and rebuilt the Globe, and it lived a long and useful life, bringing in many more pennies for another generation.

*New Place in Stratford,
bought by Shakespeare for
his family. This engraving,
from Malone's edition of
Shakespeare (1790), gives
a likeness later than that
in Shakespeare's time.*

Before the fire, and after the successful years with the Globe, Shakespeare's group added a second theater. This was a smaller indoor playhouse called Blackfriars. It seated only five or six hundred people, even a little fewer than the Mark Taper Forum at the Los Angeles Music Center. It could be lighted, performances could be given in the evening (while at the Globe they were given early in the afternoon, because of the need for daylight), and it catered to a somewhat different audience—one that could pay more than one or two pennies. It is thought that most of Shakespeare's last plays—the late romances like *Cymbeline*, *The Winter's Tale*, and *The Tempest*—were written with the Blackfriars, and its potential audience, in mind as one playhouse for their performance.

Shakespeare was very successful in all of his ventures as a professional man of the theater, he accumulated quite a lot of money, and he invested it wisely in and around Stratford. For example, he bought for his family New Place, one of the two largest dwelling houses in Stratford. He bought 107 acres of farmland, a cottage, stores of commodities (corn and malt), and a half interest in the land rentals in several villages. Having become financially independent, when he was about forty-six years old, about 1610, he moved to Stratford to be with his family—which included his wife Anne, his unmarried daughter Judith, his married daughter Susanna, her husband Dr. John Hall, and his two-year old granddaughter Elizabeth. His withdrawal from the theater didn't take long; his last two or three plays were produced within two years, and his retirement was complete by 1612. When he died, four years later, he had reached the age of only fifty-two.

III

In the nearly four centuries since that time, various people have felt compelled to assert that there was in fact no such person as Shakespeare, or (if there was) somebody else actually wrote the plays and poems attributed to him. There is some pleasant absurdity in these arguments, but they have no value as a form of truth. Shakespeare's life and activities are recorded in more than a hundred contemporary documents, and the First Folio by itself would be sufficient evidence of the existence and identity of Shakespeare, with its portrait, two corroborating poems by Ben Jonson (whose existence no one doubts), and a full explanation by the two partners who collected these thirty-six of his plays for publication.

Still, some people always want more. One dodge has been to create additional evidence by forging it. The two most active practitioners of this art, so far, have been William Henry Ireland in the eighteenth century and J. Payne Collier in the nineteenth. (If there has been an equivalent figure in the twentieth century, he or she hasn't yet come to light.) The Huntington Library has the principal holdings of the works of these two talented fabricators. (While I can't say that I have unmixed pride in this possession, at least it shows the catholicity of our stock.)

William Henry Ireland wrote, in one of his manuscript letters that we have, that "My motto is NEMO SINE VITIIS (No one without his faults)"—and I add that no one ever chose his own motto more appropriately. It could be argued that at least he was a considerate son. His father was a lover of Shakespeare and loudly lamented the absence of manuscripts of his hero. The son supplied this want by forgery. He gave his father an assortment of Shakespeare signatures and receipts, and much more. To mention only manuscripts now at the Huntington, he created a letter by Shakespeare to his wife, a poem to his wife (with a lock of his hair, which we also have), letters to the Earl of Southampton and to Richard Cowley, a new scene for *King Lear*, a new scene for *Hamlet*, and a long "Profession of Faith" in which God is likened to "the sweete Chickenne that under the coverte offe herre spredynge Wings Receyves herre lyttle Broode." Mr. Ireland Senior was very proud of his precocious son, who had performed all these marvels by the age of eighteen; even more, young Ireland created an ancestor who saved Shakespeare from drowning and was given these papers as a reward. The proud father made an exhibition of the rarities and in 1796 invited a group of notable men to see them. James Boswell was of the company, and (according to young Ireland) Boswell examined them with great care and then (after quenching his thirst with a tumbler of warm brandy and water) knelt before the documents and proclaimed, "I now kiss the invaluable relics of our bard: and thanks to God that I have lived to see them!" Fortunately, cooler, less brandied heads prevailed, and within a year or two the forgeries were exposed.

J. Payne Collier, the nineteenth-century forger, was also precocious. As he put it, he "began authorship" by the age of sixteen, and he turned out an incredible number of pamphlets, books, and editions of rare early works. Through his friendship with the Duke of Devonshire and the Earl of Ellesmere, he drew heavily on the rich resources of the Devonshire Library and the Ellesmere Collection (the Bridgewater House Library), both of which are now in the Huntington. He was a leader in learned societies and highly respected for his many contributions to learning.

He had published in the 1840s an eight-volume set of Shakespeare which went through several editions. He was dissatisfied with the possible solutions to the very kind of textual problems with which I began this essay. Consulting the Devonshire and Bridgewater House quartos and folios didn't seem to solve the problems. So he produced a copy of the Second Folio (of 1632) which was annotated throughout in a hand alleged to be of the early seventeenth century. It is known as the "Perkins Folio" because of the inscription on the leather binding, "Tho. Perkins his Booke." It includes a profusion of manuscript changes to all the plays, words added, words changed, stage directions added. For example, toward the end of *Hamlet*, Horatio says (after Hamlet's death),

> Goodnight, sweet prince,
> And flights of angels sing thee to thy rest!

Then the play concludes with some forty lines in which young Fortinbras settles the succession to the throne and marches soldiers around the stage. Collier made a quicker, more pious conclusion by having Horatio say,

> Goodnight, be blest
> And flights of angels sing thee to thy rest!

Then instead of all the soldierly business—which he scratched out —Collier wrote a new couplet to close the play:

Hora. Now cracks a Noble heart?
Goodnight ~~sweet Prince~~, & ~~aloft~~,
And flights of Angels fing thee to thy reſt,
~~Why do's the Drumme come hither?~~ ffinis

While I remaine behind to tell a tale
That shall hereafter turne the heavens pale.

While I remaine behind to tell a tale
That shall hereafter turne the heavens pale.

Which is not quite up to the request that Hamlet had made to
Horatio:

Absent thee from felicity awhile,
And in this harsh world draw thy breath in pain,
To tell my story.

But then few other writers are up to Shakespeare, distinctly not
J. Payne Collier.

Collier claimed that the annotator of the Perkins Folio had had,
from the actors in Shakespeare's company, access to better texts than
did those who collected the plays for the First Folio. Collier announced his discovery in 1852 and began publishing the results,
which created an uproar of astonishment. As soon as anyone was
allowed to examine the book, in 1859, suspicions were confirmed and
it was ultimately concluded that Collier had himself made all of these
valuable changes and additions. The Perkins Folio is now available
for examination, as it is in the Huntington Library, along with
Collier's books and about fifty of his letters in manuscript.

When Collier's forgeries were revealed, his other work was re-
examined. It was found that dozens of his other productions involved
forgery. His favorite trick was to add interlineations to authentic
texts of diaries, letters, and documents, and insert additional names
that he would wish to have found there, such as Shakespeare. Now
nothing he did can be taken at face value without careful scrutiny,
and work under suspicion is in many ways worse than no work at
all. I tell you, from personal experience, that editors often feel they
could themselves improve on the author. Fortunately, few of us put
improvement into effect by forgery.

77

IV

So we return to that collection of quartos and folios of Shakespeare's work. How did they come to be assembled here? Mr. Huntington began collecting books in the 1890s, and his tastes gradually came to be more sophisticated and his pocketbook bigger. In 1908, when he read a volume by W. Roberts called *Rare Books and Their Prices*, he wrote in the margin the names of twenty-five writers or notable books discussed in the text. One was Shakespeare, and in the text Roberts discussed the value of collecting the quartos of the plays and all four folios.

Soon the chance appeared to put this theory into practice. Among the many great libraries which Huntington acquired between 1911 and 1925, three stand out for—among many other things—their richness in Shakespeare quartos and folios. One was the E. Dwight Church Library, acquired in 1911; though it is known principally for its early Americana, it also contained some choice English literature, and about a third of our Shakespeare quartos and folios come from that collection. The acquisition of the Duke of Devonshire's Library in 1914, with its wide collection of dramatic literature, added almost another third. The purchase in 1917 of the Bridgewater House Library (the Ellesmere Collection) added another quarter to the total. Otherwise, it was one copy here and one copy there, from the F. R. Halsey Library, or Beverly Chew, or J. Marsden Perry, or from Rosenbach.

The Shakespeare collection reached preeminence in an astonishingly short time, though with much pushing from Huntington. When the international *Census of Shakespeare's Plays in Quarto* was first published, in 1916, the Huntington collection was already recorded as the largest, both in what were tabulated as "first editions" and in other early quartos. In both cases, the collection barely nosed

A collection of treasures: early quartos of Shakespeare plays from the Huntington collection.

out the British Museum, with the Bodleian Library a strong third. This was even before some of the important acquisitions, such as the Bridgewater House Library.

I have examined Mr. Huntington's copy of this census and looked at his pencilled annotations in it. He notes, for example, that those recorded as "Bridgewater" are now "Huntington." By the Perry copy of the *Merchant of Venice* of 1652 he carefully wrote "H. E. Huntington" and by a Perry *Hamlet* of 1695 he wrote "H" in the margin and "Huntington" as a reassuring footnote, should anyone not know what his "H" stood for.

When Henrietta Bartlett's more extensive bibliography of the original and early editions of Shakespeare quartos and folios—as well as of source books and contemporary notices—came out in 1922, Mr. Huntington studied the volume with great care. He put his pencil check mark to virtually every item in the 195 pages, adding a few question marks and an occasional quarrel with a date given by Bartlett.

He gave special attention to a tabulation in the front of the book, "The Key to Owners," which presented a list of owners of the greatest rarities—books of which no more than five copies were known—"arranged in the order of the number of books owned by each." Again the Huntington came first, the British Museum second, and the Bodleian third. Huntington checked each item and put totals in the margin. Then he added an additional thirteen items to his own record, and carefully inscribed the number 82 for Huntington against 67 for the British Museum and 65 for the Bodleian.

People collect for all sorts of reasons. I expect that a good part of Huntington's reason for collecting was the wish to excel, the competitive spirit, the same drive that pushed him ahead in the business world. It was the same drive that led him to say, after acquiring a small collection of early English plays, "It makes quite a reduction in the number of plays I have to secure to be even with the British Museum." In this drive to excel, book collecting can be said to have, in its motivation, a great deal in common with sports, business, and mountain climbing.

Many collectors cannot bear to part with anything they have ever acquired, just as some investors fall in love with the stocks they own, holding them in sickness and in health, so long as they both shall live. Huntington was different, in that he readily disposed of duplicate copies of rare books and specifically authorized the disposition of duplicates in the future. A series of fifteen large auction sales was held in New York between 1916 and 1924 to dispose of his duplicates for the benefit of other collectors and to raise money to buy other rarities. An effort was made to retain duplicates of special interest, among both the Shakespeare quartos and the folios. Four copies of the First Folio were kept, for example, each one of particular interest; recently a visiting scholar discovered that one of them contains a proof sheet in *King Lear*, a most unusual example that shows the corrections called for as the book was going through the press. There are also ten copies of the Second Folio, seven of the Third, and eight of the Fourth, or a total of twenty-nine copies of the seventeenth-century Shakespeare folios. In the course of the auction sales, fourteen early Shakespeare quartos were sold, all of them rare and valuable. While one looks now with longing at some that were sold, no serious mistakes seem to have been made.

A horrendous mistake *was* made at the Huntington in 1924, and it still troubles the slumbers of librarians. In the course of picking duplicates for sale, it was found that the Huntington had two copies of the first edition of Milton's *Comus*, of 1637. One copy, a beautiful, tall, untrimmed example in maroon morocco, had come from the Church Library. The other copy, much less impressive in appearance and size, and severely trimmed when it was rebound in the nineteenth century, was a Bridgewater book. So it was decided to sell the Bridgewater copy. It was noted that this copy had doubtless been in the Bridgewater Library since publication, that the book was dedicated to the Bridgewaters (before whom the masque was first performed, at their Ludlow Castle, with three children of the family taking principal parts), that this was doubtless the dedication copy, and that there were some contemporary manuscript changes in it. But it was not concluded—as bibliographers have since then thought —that the hand that made the nine manuscript corrections was the hand of John Milton, and that it was he who presented this very copy to the Bridgewaters. It is still hard to look at our beautiful, tall, maroon morocco Church copy with absolute pleasure, knowing that the other copy is elsewhere. Doubtless the memory of past mistakes is a necessary aid to humility. I trust that this one memory will suffice for our future needs.

There have, of course, been some changes in the location of copies of early Shakespeare quartos since the date of the two censuses to which I referred earlier. According to the 1976 revision of the *Short-Title Catalogue* of books printed before 1641, the Folger Shakespeare Library is now in second place behind the Huntington and ahead of the British Museum (now called the British Library) and the Bodleian in the number of early quarto editions of Shakespeare plays recorded. (There are doubtless other ways of reckoning which would produce an entirely different order, particularly if the count included duplicate copies of the same edition.) Actually, the numerical differences in the number of editions of early Shakespeare play quartos and folios in these four collections—and any consequent rankings of them—are relatively insignificant. What is significant is the fact that all four of them, two in the United States and two in England, offer magnificent facilities for scholarly research and thereby contribute handsomely to the advancement of human learning.

A collection of Shakespeare books published by the Huntington Library.

V

I began this essay with some examples of problems about the text of *Hamlet*. Those problems are still with us. It is not yet quite clear, for example, whether Hamlet sees his flesh as too too *sallied*, or too too *sullied*, or too too *solid*. But I am afraid that those who want the *solid* flesh to melt, thaw, and resolve itself into a dew are losing out in favor of *sallied* (in its meaning *soiled* or *defiled*). It may come as a disquieting surprise to be told that there are still thousands and thousands of problems outstanding in the text of Shakespeare, but it is true.

In singling out textual problems, I have meant them to be taken only as one of the many kinds of problems that scholars must still deal with. The large Huntington collections of early and rare editions of Shakespeare's works are important for many kinds of scholarship in addition to textual work. Moreover, most Shakespeare scholars can find something of value to them in our contemporaneous rare materials—books and manuscripts—of the sixteenth and seventeenth centuries, of which the Shakespeare quartos and folios are but a tiny part.

The work of literary scholarship, at least in its historical dimension, is to help us better understand plays and poems and other works of literary art by placing them in rewarding contexts. The ability to perceive those contexts requires tact, deep learning, and access to a relevant body of contemporaneous material.

The Huntington Library offers this access to scholars in most fields of English and American literature and history. As for Shakespeare scholars, they have thrived here for fifty years. I believe it is true to say that, during that time, the majority of the leading Shakespeare scholars—of this country, certainly, and of England, in good measure—have done at least some of their work here. It takes active use of an institution for it to stay alive and to serve its highest value. It is because of this active use that William Shakespeare continues to be alive at the Huntington.

The Autobiography
of
Benjamin
Franklin

About the illustrations

Over. Portrait of Franklin on an unglazed Sèvres porcelain medallion, 1778. The diameter of the original is 1⅝".

Above. Pastel portrait of Franklin attributed to Joseph Siffred Duplessis (1725-1802). The size of the original is 27" x 22¼".

Passages from the Autobiography. Various passages from the Autobiography are reproduced in facsimile in the course of the text. The passages are short extracts from the original manuscript, and most of them have been reduced in size to fit this format. The leaves of the original manuscript are about 8" wide and 13" tall; the writing in each column is about 3½" wide.

Type ornaments in margins. All of the type ornaments used in this essay are facsimiles of those used by Franklin in his printing shop in Philadelphia.

At the end of the text. Portrait of Franklin in a terracotta medallion by Jean Baptiste Nini, 1777. The diameter of the original is 4⅝".

84

B ENJAMIN FRANKLIN arrived in Philadelphia, at the Market Street Wharf, at 8 or 9 o'clock on a Sunday morning in October of 1723. He was a youth of seventeen. He had run away from his home in Boston and from his apprenticeship in the printing house of his brother James. On the last leg of a hard trip to Philadelphia, by boat, Franklin had rowed all night. That Sunday morning he was bedraggled, dirty, hungry, and sleepy. His only money was a little change. He was in working clothes, with shirts and stockings stuffed in his pocket. He knew no one, and he was looking for a job.

But first food. A baker's shop was open, and he asked for three pennyworth of any sort of bread. He was given "three great Puffy Rolls," and he walked up and down the streets eating one and holding the other two under his arms. He quenched his thirst by drinking from the river, and he gave the two rolls he couldn't eat to a woman and her child who had come in the same boat with him.

He noticed that a good many well-dressed people all seemed to be walking along in the same direction, and he fell in behind them, following them into a large house near the market. "I sat down among them," he wrote, "and after looking round a while and hearing nothing said, being very drowzy thro' Labour & want of Rest the preceding Night, I fell fast asleep, and continu'd so till the Meeting broke up, when one was kind enough to rouse me." The well-dressed people were Quakers on the way to their Sunday meeting, and Franklin had followed them into the Quaker Meeting House. "This was therefore," concluded Franklin, "the first House I was in or slept in, in Philadelphia."

Franklin tells this little episode in his Autobiography, the manuscript of which is one of the treasures of the Huntington Library.

from the Autobiography

This manuscript transmits to us one of the most esteemed works of our entire American heritage. It used to be valued, perhaps most of all, as an American success story, an epic account of a person who rises from rags to riches: the inside story of how a poor boy becomes a top leader in the worlds of government, intellect, and science through the exercise of a few plain virtues. To modern eyes, the Autobiography may seem to be the story of a man in search of his self, a narrative of accomplishments set against the candid revelation of motives and of the private inner life. It has many different appeals and many different charms.

An exploration of this notable work may lead us to a better understanding of the Autobiography and to a deeper appreciation of the kind of man that Franklin was. Then we can consider why and how Franklin happened to write these remembrances of time long past, the wandering travels that this adventurous manuscript had, like Ulysses, and how it came at last to find a safe harbor and home at the Huntington Library, full of honor and years.

II

Openness is a great virtue in itself, and in what it can lead to. One of the prime qualities of Franklin's Autobiography is its sense of openness. Franklin gives the impression of writing with the perfect candor that one hopes for from a close friend. He doesn't put on airs, and he seems to be out there in full view of everyone. If you care to look at any of his sides, all the way around, there he is. He is the plain American who wore an old fur cap in France when the men with whom he mingled were all wearing powdered wigs; and he kept those funny metal-framed bifocal glasses perched on his nose, no matter how odd they seemed to the elegant.

Franklin uses plain language, and he tells us the little details that are the texture of living. When he was the clerk of the Pennsylvania Assembly, he had to sit and listen (he says) to all the debates which were "often so unentertaining that I was induc'd to amuse myself with making magic Squares, or Circles, or anything to avoid Weariness." Franklin portrays himself as a doodler, keeping busy "to avoid Weariness." As a young fellow he wrote poetry, which he was willing to characterize as "wretched Stuff." He doesn't mind telling that, as a student, he "acquired fair Writing pretty soon, but I fail'd in the Arithmetic, and made no Progress in it." He freely admits his "Intrigues with Low Women that fell in my Way."

With this openness, we have the feeling that he is free to write about anything and everything, his likes and his dislikes. He was, for example, critical of drinking — or "Dramming" as he commonly called it. He said, with some disgust, that the workmen in a London printing house where he worked were "great Guzzlers of Beer," as each of them thought it was necessary "to drink strong Beer that he might be *strong* to labour." But "the 'Water-American'" (as they called him) tried to convince them that "the Bodily Strength afforded by Beer could only be in proportion to the Grain or Flour of the Barley dissolv'd in the Water of which it was made; that there was more Flour in a Penny-worth of Bread, and therefore if he would eat that with a Pint of Water, it would give him more Strength than a Quart of Beer." But his argument didn't convince the printers.

Neither could he convince the Indians on this point. Franklin was sent as a commissioner to make a treaty with the Indians at Carlisle. "As those People are extreamly apt to get drunk," he wrote, "and when so are very quarrelsome and disorderly, we strictly forbad the selling any Liquor to them; and when they complain'd of this restriction, we told them that if they would continue sober during the Treaty, we would give them Plenty of Rum when Business was over." The promises were all kept, and the Indians spent the night after the conclusion of the business getting roaring drunk, building bonfires, yelling and fighting, and keeping everybody awake. The next morning the Indians sent three old counselors to apologize. "The Orator acknowledg'd the Fault," wrote Franklin, "but laid it upon the Rum; and then endeavour'd to excuse the Rum, by saying, *'The great Spirit who made all things made every thing for some use, and whatever Use he design'd any thing for, that Use it should always be put to; Now, when he made Rum, he said* LET THIS BE FOR INDIANS TO GET DRUNK WITH. And it must be so.'" Franklin added that if it was the design of Providence to get rid of the Indians, "it seems not improbable that Rum may be the appointed Means."

Throughout the Autobiography, Franklin seems to be trying to get to the heart of whatever matter he speaks of. The sense of openness suggests a freedom to speak with absolute candor. He is always trying to find a way to understand other people. His way is to observe and to verbalize his perceptions in a few words. One man he said was "of uncommon natural parts, and great wit and humor, but a little idle." Another was "lively, witty, good natur'd, and a pleasant Companion; but idle, thoughtless, and imprudent to the last degree." A man for whom he worked was, he thought, "an odd Fish, ignorant of common Life, fond of rudely opposing receiv'd Opinions, slovenly to extream dirtiness, enthusiastic in some Points of Religion, and a little Knavish withal."

The chief character in an autobiography is, of course, the writer himself. That is the person we want to get to know. That was the same person whom Franklin was trying to get to know — and to reveal to himself as well as to the reader — when he was writing this manuscript. I have been calling attention to the openness, or freedom with which he treated topics. That freedom extends to the treatment of himself. Let us now consider what kind of man Franklin reveals himself to be in his Autobiography.

III

Franklin appears as an ambitious and industrious man who makes the best of his own talents. He had a wit and humor often lacking in the makeup of ambitious people, and he had the charm of feeling that constant good fortune had accompanied him throughout his life. In answer to that question which everyone faces at one time or another—would you like to live your same life over again—he could answer without hesitation, "I should have no Objections to a Repetition of the same life from its Beginning, only asking the Advantage Authors have in a second Edition to correct some Faults of the first."

Of the six men who are usually called the Founding Fathers, Franklin was the most senior in age, and eminent before any of the others had any public accomplishments at all. He was twenty-six when George Washington (the next eldest) was born, fifty-one at the time of the birth of Alexander Hamilton, the youngest of the six. John Adams, Thomas Jefferson, and James Madison fall between those two. Franklin served with all six of them throughout the long revolutionary period, and he was often regarded as the wise senior counselor. He could be counted on to guide a successful course through the dangers that beset the bold adventurers who established this republic.

Of all the Founding Fathers, however, Franklin was the only one who had had almost no formal education. John Adams graduated from Harvard, Thomas Jefferson from William and Mary, James Madison from Princeton (then called the College of New Jersey), Alexander Hamilton from King's College (now Columbia). Even George Washington had eight years of formal schooling plus practical training in surveying, tobacco growing, and stock raising—training suitable for a gentleman as preparation for running a Virginia estate.

On the other hand, Benjamin Franklin was in grammar school for less than a year, and he had other part-time lessons for only one year. At the age of ten, his academic training was over. But not his learning. "From a Child," he tells us in the Autobiography, "I was fond of Reading, and all the little Money that came into my Hands was ever laid out in Books." As an apprentice, he used to borrow books overnight through the stealthy kindness of apprentices of booksellers. "Often I sat up in my Room reading the greatest Part of the Night," he said, "when the Book was borrow'd in the Evening and to be return'd early in the Morning, lest it should be miss'd or wanted." He was deeply informed in a great variety of subjects. He was especially pleased to be given honorary degrees by both Harvard and Yale, and he observed: "Thus without studying in any College I came to partake of their Honours."

Of the six Founding Fathers, all except Franklin came from privileged and well-to-do families. Franklin's father made tallow candles and soap, and Franklin was the fifteenth of seventeen children, and the tenth boy. His father tried to have, at the dinner table, "some sensible Friend or Neighbour, to converse with, and always took care to start some ingenious or useful Topic for Discourse, which might tend to improve the Minds of his Children." As a result, Franklin said he took no notice of the food—"Whether it was well or ill drest, in or out of season, of good or bad flavour"—and found this habit of "perfect Inattention to those Matters" a great convenience to him the rest of his life. He may not have been a very rewarding guest for some hostesses, but at least he did not have to share the occasional unhappiness of those with "more delicate because better instructed Tastes and Appetites," as he traveled about the world.

Various trades were open to Franklin, and his father taught him candlemaking, a trade which Franklin disliked. Franklin wanted to go to sea, but that was a trade which his father disliked for him. So they compromised on printing, and that was how he came to be apprenticed to his elder brother.

Franklin turned out to be a successful printer, and he made a good living from his trade, which he kept extending in Philadelphia to include a shop, a newspaper, and the publication of Poor Richard's Almanac. The trade of printing was not very high in the ordinary scale of prestige, as it was a craft rather than a profession. But Franklin thought of himself, throughout his life, as a printer first of all, and he commenced his last will and testament with the words, "I, Benjamin Franklin, Printer...."

The Autobiography is full of printer's language. Every mistake is called an "erratum," and his life was (in his view) peppered with "errata." One of "the great Errata of my Life," he says, was failing to write more than one letter to Deborah Read during the two years of his first trip to England. Although they had had a kind of under-

Deborah Read Franklin
in a contemporary
engraving

standing looking toward matrimony, she married someone else during his extended and silent absence. That man already had a wife in England, however, and he also deserted Deborah by running away to the West Indies to evade his creditors. So, in due course, as Franklin wrote, "I took her to Wife. . . . She prov'd a good and faithful Helpmate, assisted me much by attending the Shop, we throve together and ever mutually endeavour'd to make each other happy. Thus I corrected that great Erratum as well as I could."

Franklin used the language of his trade on every kind of occasion. He did so in a half-humorous, half-serious epitaph that he composed for himself when he was only twenty-eight, and which is well worth repeating:

THE BODY OF
B. FRANKLIN,
PRINTER;
LIKE THE COVER OF AN OLD BOOK,
ITS CONTENTS TORN OUT,
AND STRIPT OF ITS LETTERING & GILDING,
LIES HERE, FOOD FOR WORMS.
BUT THE WORK SHALL NOT BE WHOLLY LOST:
FOR IT WILL, AS HE BELIEV'D, APPEAR ONCE MORE,
IN A NEW & MORE PERFECT EDITION,
CORRECTED AND AMENDED
BY THE AUTHOR.

It is, I suppose, the most famous epitaph ever written, with the witty view and the sentimental view just about balancing one another off.

The trade of printer involved setting type, operating the printing press, and selling the results. The trade, as Franklin conceived it, also included writing a good deal of what was to be printed, in the almanacs, the pamphlets, and the newspapers. To carry out that part of the task, he had to teach himself to write. One of his ways — which he describes in the Autobiography — was to imitate the prose of Addison and Steele. He came by an odd volume of the *Spectator*, read it with delight and admiration, and tried to teach himself to write their way. "I took some of the Papers," he said, "and by making short Hints of the Sentiment in each Sentence, laid them by a few Days, and then without looking at the Book, try'd to compleat the Papers again, by expressing each hinted Sentiment at length and as fully as it had been express'd before, in any suitable Words that should come to hand. Then I compar'd my *Spectator* with the Original, discover'd some of my Faults, and corrected them." He also "took some of the Tales & turn'd them into Verse: And after a time, when I had pretty well forgotten the Prose, turn'd them back again. I also sometimes jumbled my Collections of Hints into Confusion, and after some Weeks, endeavour'd to reduce them into the best

from the Autobiography

Order, before I began to form the full Sentences and compleat the Paper. This was to teach me Method in the Arrangement of Thoughts. By comparing my Work afterwards with the original, I discover'd many faults and amended them." And he learned to write, very well indeed.

On the whole, the Founding Fathers were a very productive lot of writers. Franklin certainly outdid them all in quantity of publishing, and in the range and variety of his subjects — from scientific papers to salty humor, from political essays to drinking songs. And perhaps he outdid all the others in clarity, grace, and wit. Also, he was a fast writer. On one trip from England to Philadelphia, he wrote three of his longest pamphlets: one on navigation, one on smoky chimneys, and one on his smoke-consuming stove. When he disembarked, they were ready for the press.

Franklin and John Adams were on the committee with Thomas Jefferson to draft the Declaration of Independence. Jefferson actually wrote the Declaration, of course, and submitted it to the other two, who made only verbal changes. Franklin made half a dozen changes, but one little sample may reveal a good deal about Franklin. Jefferson had written: "We hold these truths to be sacred and undeniable" —thus basing the truths on religion and on logic. Franklin changed it to: "We hold these truths to be self-evident" — thus basing the truths on common human experience rather than on religion and logic. It was *common human experience* to which he turned for a firm basis; the *senses, observation,* and *experiment* were his guides, and *useful* and *pleasing* were his goals.

Franklin taught himself to write, and to him nothing appeared impossible. He was a great solver of problems. A zealous Presbyterian chaplain of the Pennsylvania militia once complained to Franklin, while they were building forts in the western part of the state, that the soldiers "did not generally attend his Prayers and Exhortations." Franklin—who himself always avoided church services when he could—observed that the soldiers were very punctual in receiving their ration of a gill of rum a day, half in the morning and half in the evening. He said to the chaplain, "'It is perhaps below the Dignity of your Profession to act as Steward of the Rum. But if you were to deal it out, and only just after Prayers, you would have them all about you.' He lik'd the Thought, undertook the Office,

from the
Autobiography

and with the help of a few hands to measure out the Liquor executed it to Satisfaction; and never were Prayers more generally and more punctually attended."

How to get the best speed out of sailing ships is another example of a problem that intrigued him. He noticed that there was no uniformity in loading, rigging, and sailing a ship. "I think a Set of Experiments might be instituted," he wrote, "first to determine the most proper Form of the Hull for swift sailing; next the best Dimensions and properest Place for the Masts; then the Form and Quantity of Sail, and their Position as the Winds may be; and lastly the Disposition of her Lading. This is the Age of Experiments; and such a Set accurately made and combin'd would be of great Use. I am therefore persuaded that erelong some ingenious Philosopher will undertake it: — to whom I wish Success."

He was interested in every practical question. How to fight the Indians, for example: he quickly saw the error in General Braddock's plan to capture Fort Duquesne and march "the King's regular and disciplin'd Troops" (of which he was so confident) on to Niagara and Frontenac; Franklin tactfully pointed the error out to Braddock, who "smil'd at my Ignorance" — even though Franklin had already proved his singular reliability by supplying the transport wagons

from the
Autobiography.
Franklin's summary
comment on
General Braddock

I was concern'd, I therefore before I left Frederick desired Mr. Franklin, Post master of Pensilvana, and a Man of great Influence in that Province to contract for 150 Waggons and a Number of Horses, which he has executed with great punctuality & Integrity, and is almost the only Instance of Ability & honesty I have known in these provinces; His Waggons & Horses have all joind me, and are indeed my whole Dependance

Above. Portion of a letter from General Braddock to Sir Thomas Robinson, June 5, 1755, from "Fort Cumberland at Will's Creek." In this part of his official report of the preparations for the attack on Fort Duquesne, Braddock tells (from his point of view) of the dealings with Franklin. Compare Franklin's views (left) of the same enterprise.

Below. Letter from Deborah Franklin in Philadelphia to Peter Collinson, merchant, in London, April 30, 1755. A wife's comment on her husband's work as described (above) by General Braddock and (in the text) by her husband.

Sir

Mr. Franklin is from home, and can not have by this Conveyance an Opportunity of answering yr. Favours by the last Ships. I have forwarded yr. Letters to Mr. Elliot, Mr. Bartram, Mr. Barton and Mr. Franklin. My Husband is now in the Back Counties, contracting for some Waggons and Horses for the Army, which tho' so much out of his Way, he was obliged to undertake, for preventing some Inconveniencies that might have attended so many raw Hands sent us from Europe, who are not accustomed to necesary Affairs.

I am very sincerly & truly

Yr. very sincere Friend & humble Servt.

Philada.
Aprl. 30. 1755

Deborah Franklin

and horses that Braddock needed. Likewise, Franklin turned his attention to the practical question of how to sweep city streets. He watched a feeble old woman at work, and devised one method for the summer and another for the winter, deciding on the number of gutters and the best kind of cart for carrying away the sweepings. "Some may think these trifling Matters not worth minding or relating," he wrote; but his conclusion was summed up in the aphorism that "Human Felicity is produc'd not so much by great Pieces of good Fortune that seldom happen, as by little Advantages that occur every Day. Thus if you teach a poor young Man to shave himself and keep his Razor in order, you may contribute more to the Happiness of his Life than in giving him 1000 Guineas."

Franklin stands at the very head of the How-To-Do-It school. The Autobiography is sprinkled with suggestions. How to turn an enemy into a friend. How to build a wharf. How to appear as industrious as you really are. How to establish your own religion. How to start a swimming school. How to dispute without being disagreeable. How to raise money for good causes. And the like.

Franklin was a man who truly believed that things need not be the way they are. Not only in changing the external world of nature for the benefit of man, but also in changing the world within man. "I conceiv'd," he wrote, "the bold and arduous Project of arriving at moral Perfection. I wish'd to live without committing any Fault at any time." He did not find the help he needed in the church, and he even planned to establish a new church — but that was a project that he did not prosecute, though he wrote a liturgy for his own use. Instead, he proceeded to make a list of the moral virtues that he wanted to master, and he set them down in the order in which he wanted to master them, for their value in contributing to the mastery of other virtues. *Temperance* stood first in his list, followed by *Silence, Order,* and *Resolution;* then *Frugality, Industry, Sincerity,* and *Justice;* then *Moderation, Cleanliness,* and *Tranquillity;* and lastly, in twelfth place, *Chastity.* A Quaker friend told him, he wrote, "that I was generally thought proud; that my Pride show'd itself frequently in Conversation; that I was not content with being in the right when discussing any Point, but was overbearing and rather insolent; of which he convinc'd me by mentioning several Instances; — I determined endeavouring to cure myself if I could of this Vice or Folly among the rest, and I added *Humility* to my List, giving an extensive Meaning to the Word." (Actually, the "Meaning" he gave was, "Imitate Jesus and Socrates" — which is extensive enough, though perhaps confusing to most imitators.)

It is hard to know how well he succeeded in learning humility by imitating Jesus and Socrates. One of Franklin's charms is his vanity, that younger sister of pride. Dozens of times in the Autobiography, innocent vanity comes popping out. "Most People dislike Vanity in others," he wrote, "whatever Share they have of it themselves, but

94

I give it fair Quarter wherever I meet with it, being persuaded that it is often productive of Good to the Possessor and to others that are within his Sphere of Action: And therefore in many Cases it would not be quite absurd if a Man were to thank God for his Vanity among the other Comforts of Life." (It would be hard to dislike a man who looks at the world with such amused perceptiveness.)

The trouble is that vanity is always wanting to grow up and become pride. And Franklin never claims to have conquered pride, despite his daily practice of what might be called moral calisthenics. "In reality," he wrote, "there is perhaps no one of our natural Passions so hard to subdue as *Pride*. Disguise it, struggle with it, beat it down, stifle it, mortify it as much as one pleases, it is still alive, and will every now and then peep out and show itself. You will see it perhaps often in this History [his Autobiography]. For even if I could conceive that I had compleatly overcome it, I should probably be proud of my humility."

But Franklin did work hard at improving his moral virtue. His first step was to rule sheets of paper with columns for the days of the week and lines for each virtue. Then he graded himself on each day's performance for each virtue, using a series of checks and rotat-

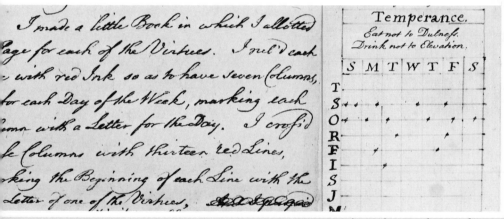

from the Autobiography

ing the order of the virtues. Franklin was nothing if not a man of method, and he would have been at home in systems analysis. He found it difficult, however, not to give up the struggle and be satisfied with his method, or with a little improvement instead of persevering for a more complete improvement, and he compared his situation to the man who liked a speckled ax best. Here is the story, as he told it. A "Man who in buying an Ax of a Smith my Neighbour, desired to have the whole of its Surface as bright as the Edge; the Smith consented to grind it bright for him if he would turn the

Wheel. He turn'd while the Smith press'd the broad Face of the Ax hard & heavily on the Stone, which made the Turning of it very fatiguing. The Man came every now & then from the Wheel to see how the Work went on; and at length would take his Ax as it was without farther Grinding. 'No,' says the Smith, 'Turn on, turn on; we shall have it bright by and by; as yet 'tis only speckled.' 'Yes,' says the Man; *but I think I like a speckled Ax best.'*" I do not know whether Franklin got beyond the speckled stage in his moral improvement, but he certainly turned the wheel a lot.

He also planned each day's program and made a little chart for his Autobiography showing his schedule from 5 a.m. (when he is to "Rise, wash, and address *Powerful Goodness*") until he retires at 10 p.m. (after his "Examination of the Day"). The Autobiography is usually open on exhibition to the pages which contain this chart, which is one of the best-known passages in it, with a pervasive later influence. F. Scott Fitzgerald made ironic use of this same kind of chart in *The Great Gatsby*: the hero, as a child, had a similar sched-

Left. Franklin's chart from the Autobiography, giving his daily schedule
Below: Gatsby's daily schedule, from Fitzgerald's *The Great Gatsby*

Rise from bed	6.00	A. M.
Dumbbell exercise and wall-scaling	6.15–6.30	"
Study electricity, etc....................	7.15–8.15	"
Work.................................	8.30–4.30	P. M.
Baseball and sports.....................	4.30–5.00	"
Practice elocution, poise and how to attain it	5.00–6.00	"
Study needed inventions.................	7.00–9.00	"

GENERAL RESOLVES

No wasting time at Shafters or [a name, indecipherable]
No more smokeing or chewing.

Bath every other day
Read one improving book or magazine per week
Save $5.00 [crossed out] $3.00 per week
Be better to parents

ule — including "rise from bed" at 6:00 a.m., "study needed inventions" for two hours before retiring at 9:00 p.m., and (among his General Resolves) "bath every other day" and "read one improving book or magazine per week." Gatsby's dream of success took a different course from Franklin's dream of moral perfection: Gatsby became a successful criminal, and Fitzgerald turns the knife of satire in his dream, superficially so like that of Franklin's. The dream of improvement and the vision of success still are around, and they can be directed to any kind of end.

For Franklin, the final end was mainly public service. His scientific studies led to various useful discoveries, including the lightning rod, the Franklin stove, and bifocal glasses. His energies of persuasion resulted in his fellow citizens joining with him to form the American Philosophical Society, the Library Company of Philadelphia, a hospital, a fire company, a police force, an insurance company, a militia, and an academy which became the University of Pennsylvania. And he was also a notable public figure: a clerk of the Pennsylvania legislature when he was young, then postmaster of Philadelphia, deputy postmaster general, agent in London for the colony of Pennsylvania, delegate to the Second Continental Congress, commissioner to France during the Revolution, representative to conclude the War and sign the treaty with Great Britain, and a member of the Constitutional Convention. When Franklin died in 1790, at the age of eighty-four, the United States was well launched

"Franklin before the Privy Council," an oil painting dated 1857 by Christian Schussele (1824-1879), 57½" by 85¼". In this dramatic scene, imaginatively reconstructed, Franklin is being examined (in January 1774, in London) about the publication of some letters said to relate to the rights of the colonists; the Lord President of the Privy Council is in the chair.

on the course of its history as a republic, and he had had a major share in that launching.

The Autobiography concludes when Franklin was about fifty-two, in 1758, before his greatest fame. But the Autobiography is mainly about Franklin as a man, anyway, not as a public figure. About what he was like, more than what he achieved. About his own sense of himself, more than what others thought of him. And in all these ways his Autobiography can speak to each one of us who have ambitions and dreams, no matter what our role in the world may be. At the same time, the Autobiography is the model of the great American dream of success.

Franklin was sixty-five years old when he first began to write what we call his Autobiography, what he called his Memoirs. I would like to give a short account of the composition of the Auto-biography, for the light it may throw on our understanding of it and of Franklin.

In 1771, when he was sixty-five, he had been living in London for six years, as agent for the Colony of Pennsylvania (as well as of Georgia, New Jersey, and Massachusetts). In August of 1771 he was invited to visit a friend, Jonathan Shipley, a Bishop of the Church of England, who had a country house in Twyford, near the

Folding his page lengthwise into two equal columns, Franklin wrote his first draft very rapidly in the right-hand column, leaving the rest of the page blank for adding afterthoughts and revisions. Almost every one of the 230 pages shows additions of this kind. The addition on the left-hand side of page one shown here covered two blank columns, and Franklin used arrows to show where it should come in his final draft. His penmanship and ink show that he made some revisions, both between the lines and in the blank spaces, many years after composing the first draft. The heading here, "Twyford, at the Bishop of St. Asaph's 1771," was added in 1788. Of about sixty such late revisions, a half-dozen could have been added as Franklin lay dying in 1790.

southern coast of England. There Bishop Shipley lived with his wife, one son (away at the time), and five daughters ranging in age from eleven to twenty-three. There Franklin began to write his Autobiography. He took some large sheets of paper, folded each one once, and put them together as a loose gathering. He treated each page as if it had space for two columns, and he wrote only in one column, wisely leaving the other column blank for additional thoughts, revisions, and corrections.

He began the Autobiography in the form of a long letter to his illegitimate son, William Franklin, who was then royal governor of New Jersey, and for his posterity. He commences the story with an informal account of some of his predecessors and moves on to his own childhood and youth and early maturity; this part breaks off at the year 1730, when he was twenty-four, at the time of his marriage to Deborah Read.

Franklin wrote carefully, and revised as he went along. In introducing his father into the narrative, he first wrote, "Perhaps you may like to know something of his Character," but this sentence did not suit him and he changed it to read, "I think you may like to know something of his Person & Character." Similarly, in describing his experience in his daily accounting of his striving for moral perfection, he wrote: "I enter'd upon this Plan for Self Examination, and continu'd it for some time"; but he felt the need to make the statement more precise and added two phrases so that his sentence became: "I enter'd upon the Execution of this Plan for Self Examination, and continu'd it with occasional Intermissions for some time." His revisions are generally in the direction of greater precision or more specific detail. In telling of his first arrival in Philadelphia and

and the Journey I took for that purpose.
> Now imagining it may be equally
~~& some of~~
agreable to you to know the Circumstances of my Life, ~~before your Time,~~ many of which you are yet unacquainted with; and expecting a Weeks uninterrupted Leisure in my present Country Retirement, I sit down to write them for you. ~~r Perusal Use~~ To which I have besides some other Inducements. Having emerg'd
the
from Poverty & Obscurity in which I was born & bred, to a State of Affluence & some Degree of ~~Fame~~ Reputation
∧in the World, ~~the Means I made~~

Twyford at the Bishop
of St Asaph's
Dear Son,   1770.
        I have ever had a Pleasure in
any
obtaining ~~In~~ little ~~traditionary Anec~~ Anecdotes of my Ancestors. You may remember the Enquiries I made among the Remains of my Relations when you were with me in England.;
> [The Notes ~~my U~~ one of my Uncles ~~left me~~ (who had the same kind of ~~in searching~~ collecting Family Anecdotes) Curiosity∧once put into my Hands, furnish'd me with several Particulars., relating to our ~~Family Progenitors~~ Ancestors.
        Notes
∧From the~~mose~~∧ I learnt that the Family had liv'd in the same Village, Ecton in Northamptonshire, for 300

of walking the streets in a bedraggled condition, he added (in the blank column), "passing by the Door of Mr Read, my future Wife's Father, when she standing at the Door saw me, & thought I made as I certainly did a most awkward ridiculous Appearance." But sometimes his second thoughts are as extensive as his first ones, and they fill the entire blank column.

This first part of the Autobiography occupies eighty-seven manuscript pages and is the homeliest and most charming part of the entire work. Franklin seems to have been carried away in giving a personal account of his boyhood adventures, and he appears to have relished his role as a storyteller. There is a tradition that Franklin wrote for several hours each day and then read that installment to the Shipley family in the evening.

Franklin returned to London, set aside his manuscript, and did not return to the project for thirteen years, not until the year 1784, when he was seventy-eight years old. In the meantime, the American Revolution had taken place, his son had—to Franklin's great sadness—gone over to the British side and was estranged from his father, and the trunk containing the manuscript and some of Franklin's other papers and books had been broken into in Philadelphia during the British occupation of the city in 1777-78. In 1782, the manuscript was found by the executor of the estate of the widow of the man to whom Franklin had entrusted his trunk—a dear friend named Joseph Galloway, who also had gone over to the British side. The executor, Abel James, wrote in 1782 to Franklin in France, where he was on the commission sent to seek French help, told him of the discovery, enclosed a copy of Franklin's original outline of the Autobiography, and urged him to continue the project. Franklin wrote to an English friend, Benjamin Vaughan, who had recently published an edition of Franklin's writings in London, and asked his advice. Vaughan was most enthusiastic. But it was not until two years later that Franklin resumed the writing of his Autobiography. He was still living in France, but he undertook to continue his account even though he did not have his private papers with him. He decided to make a statement of his ideals and to set forth what he had done that he thought most important in shaping his character. He set forth his ideas in twenty-seven pages, mainly describing his early scheme for achieving moral perfection through practicing the thirteen virtues.

Soon he returned to Philadelphia, in 1785, but he did not resume work on his Autobiography again until August of 1788, when he was eighty-two. In the meantime he had not been idle: he had been president of the Supreme Executive Council of Pennsylvania (governor, other states called it), and he had been a member of the Federal Constitutional Convention. The third part, written in 1788, is a long section, of 120 pages, that carries his life down to the age of fifty-one, in the year of 1757. Then he set the Autobiography aside

Above. Franklin tells candidly how he gained "Credit and Character as a Tradesman."
In order to secure my Credit and Character as a Tradesman, I took care not only to be in Reality Industrious & frugal, but to avoid all Appearances of the Contrary. I drest plainly; I frequent I was seen at no Places of idle Diversion; I never went out a fishing or shooting;

Below. Franklin explains one of his principles in dealing with people.
Assertion of my own. I even forbid myself the Use of every Word or Expression in the Language that imported a fix'd Opinion; such as certainly, undoubtedly, &c. and I adopted instead of them, I conceive, I apprehend, or I imagine a thing to be so or so, When another asserted something, that I thought in Error, I deny'd my self the Pleasure of contradicting him

yet once more, for almost two further years. In the last year of his life, 1789-90, when he was eighty-four, he wrote a fourth and last section (of some nine pages) which covers only about a year. There the Autobiography ends with its writer fifty-two years old, in 1758, and most of his great triumphs still in front of him in the last thirty-two years of his life.

But this is not the end of the story of the travels of the manuscript of the Autobiography. It still had to cross the Atlantic twice and become lost once more. In 1785, between the writing of parts two and three, Franklin decided to revise what he had already written. He read it through and made various alterations, adding a title of a book here, changing a date there. These later changes seemed mostly to be intended to improve the accuracy and to increase the detail, though sometimes the later perspective leads him to new views.

In the process of making revisions, both in the course of the initial writings and in later reviews, Franklin added a great deal both between the lines and in the blank columns, as a glance at the manuscript reveals. Thanks to the blank columns, all of his original and later and much later thoughts are preserved for us, and the manuscript provides a running record of them in permanent form. The record is generally complicated, and sometimes illegible. Once a bottle of ink turned over on the manuscript, and the result—very accurately called the "black page"—has been much photographed in attempts to recover his words from its inky depth.

In any event, Franklin proceeded, in 1788, to write the third part. In 1789, he had his grandson, Benjamin Franklin Bache, make two copies of the revised manuscript, and he sent one to Benjamin Vaughan in London and the other to Louis Guillaume Le Veillard, mayor of the town of Passy in France, where Franklin had lived. He sought their advice about publication, and asked that no part of the manuscript be copied for any purpose whatsoever.

Franklin retained the original manuscript, added the fourth part, and then died in 1790. His grandson, Temple Franklin, who was willed all of his grandfather's books and papers, set out for London in 1791 bearing (among other things) the original Autobiography. He was distressed to find that a French translation had already been printed, and two different English versions of the Autobiography were soon also printed by translating the French back to English. These retranslations, remote from the original, were reprinted many times and accepted as authentic.

Temple Franklin went to France and swapped his precious original manuscript of the Autobiography for Le Veillard's incomplete copy. Temple Franklin was presumably unaware of the unique fourth part or the rich maze of Franklin's second and third thoughts, and he must have assumed that Le Veillard's copy would have been easier for a printer to deal with. In any event, that copy was lost, and also the copy which had been sent to Vaughan. The printed versions in

The "black page" of the Autobiography. Overturning an early bottle of ink made this problem for scholars.

... had scarce opened our Letters & put
our Press in Order before George Houfe, an
Acquaintance of mine, brought a Countryman
to us, whom he had met in the
Street enquiring for a Printer: All
... was now expended in the
... the Particulars we had
... this Countryman's
... being our First Fruits
... sonably, gave me more
... in the mercantry Courfe. I have
... and has made me
... than perhaps I
... have been to afsist
... Beginnings

... have mentioned before,
... Women of the preceding
... had form'd most of my
... Acquaintance into a
... Improvement
... which we call'd the Junto.
... on Friday Evening: The
... required that every
... Turn fould produce
... Queries on any Point of
... or Natural Philoso
... by the Company,
... once in three Month,
... and read an Efsay of
... on any Subject.
... Our Debates were to
... Direction of a Prefident
... conducted in the fincere
... Enquiry after Truth, without
... or Difire of Vi
... Philadelphia was c
... already half Bank
... and all Appear
... new Buildings & the Rife of
... being to his certain Kn
... for they were inf
... Things that would foon
... he gave me fuch a Deta
... now existing or that
... that he left me half m
... known him before I am
... probably, I fould ann
... have done it. This Ma
... to live in
... in the same St
... to buy a Houfe the

all editions for many years derived from incomplete copies which are now lost. Of the manuscripts, only the original remained, in France, in the hands of Le Veillard, who was busy making a careful French translation of it. But in 1794, Le Veillard lost his head to the guillotine in the Reign of Terror. The manuscript of the Autobiography went to his grandnephew by marriage and dropped out of sight for almost seventy-five years.

John Bigelow, the U.S. Minister to France in 1865-66, found it after a search, bought it in 1867, and brought it home again. When Bigelow printed the Autobiography from the original manuscript in 1868, it was the first time that the complete text had ever been printed, but even then very imperfectly. Bigelow kept the manuscript for some thirty years and then sold it to Dodd, Mead and Company, booksellers in New York. Dodd Mead sold it to E. Dwight Church, who was a great New York book collector and identified in a contemporary newspaper as "a wealthy manufacturer of soda, the senior member of Church and Dwight of New York."

The library that E. Dwight Church assembled was described by Luther S. Livingston, in a fit of enthusiasm, as "the choicest and most valuable collection ever brought together." Although it contained only some 2,133 items when the catalogs of the library were printed in 1907 and 1909, it consisted mainly of notable books and manuscripts. The catalog of the Americana material ran to five fat volumes and supplied good company for Franklin's Autobiography. For example, it included the following books and manuscripts, which will be familiar to those who have followed exhibitions at the Huntington Library over the years. *The Book of the General Lawes and Libertyes Concerning the Inhabitants of the Massachusets* (1648), the only surviving copy of a landmark in American legal history, the first collection of laws printed in this country. The Bay Psalm Book (1640), the first English book written and printed in the New World, and the first book of any sort printed in the English colonization of the Americas. The Eliot Indian Bible (1663), John Eliot's translation of the Bible into the language of the Massachusetts Indians, the first Bible printed in this country. George Washington's manuscript account of the genealogy of his family, written by him in 1792 while he was president. The material in the other Church catalog (of two volumes, called English Literature and Miscellanea) is equally impressive. There were, for example, nine splendid Books of Hours (illuminated manuscripts, on vellum, French and Flemish of the fifteenth and early sixteenth centuries); and the Shakespeare collection, one of the finest holdings in the world, included eleven copies of the first four folios, thirteen first quartos of individual plays, fifteen second quartos, and twenty-seven other early quartos.

After Church's death, the executors of his estate planned to sell his Library at auction, but Henry E. Huntington intervened and, in April of 1911, bought the entire collection for $750,000. The president of the Anderson Auction Company of New York wrote him a generous letter of congratulations. "Dear Mr. Huntington:—I congratulate you most sincerely on the purchase of the Church Library. I had hoped that it would be sold by us at auction but it is really much better that you should have it, if the Library is to be kept intact, at least the absolutely unique collection of Americana, by far the most important in the world in this department."

The Church Library was the first major collection that Huntington acquired, and it served as a pattern for some of his most significant later acquisitions. An editorial writer in the New York *Tribune* said, after the purchase of the Church Library, that Huntington "is now riding his hobby as a collector of books at full tilt." Little did the writer realize that the Church Library was only the first of a dozen libraries of comparable importance that would be acquired, along with hundreds of smaller collections, and thousands of individual items. Together they would form the nucleus of the ever-growing Huntington Library, one of the world's great resources for the advancement of learning by scholars of British and American history and literature and greater understanding for the world at large.

The original check list for the delivery of the Church Library in 1911 bears the following annotation by the side of the Autobiography of Benjamin Franklin: "delivered to Mr Huntington." This manuscript was then considered a special treasure, and ever since it has been regarded as one of the treasures of the Huntington Library. It has been studied by many scholars seeking to follow, through its tremendously complex system of revisions and substitutions and alterations, some further clues toward an understanding of Franklin's mind and of his intentions—questions which have not yet been fully answered. It has been looked at by thousands of visitors seeking to come into closer contact with one of the greatest of our Founding Fathers. It can stand as a fine symbol to commemorate the American heritage from the eighteenth century.

WILLIAM BLAKE
the Power of the Imagination

About the illustrations

Over. The drawing, by Blake, depicts the conversion of Saul. It was drawn about 1800, in pen and watercolor; the size of the original is 16⅛″ by 14⅛″.

Above. This portrait of Blake is an engraving by L. Schiavonetti after a painting by T. Phillips. The example reproduced is a folio proof copy for its first appearance, as the frontispiece to the illustrated edition of Robert Blair's *The Grave* (1808).

Facing page. The Swinburne quotation is from the manuscript for his *William Blake: A Critical Essay* (1868).

Visionary Heads. The pencil drawings shown in the margins (in reduced size) are from a series of nine imaginary portraits by Blake in the Huntington collection.

The genius of William Blake—&his genius is one with character: at one with it on all points &in every way is so peculiar a charm that no one not incapable of ling its fascination can ever outlive his delight in it.

A. C. Swinburne, 1867

Genius is awe-inspiring and mysterious. It is hard to account for and impossible to explain. I mean by genius the highly creative and deeply original talent that can give the world something of unusual value, radically different in kind or in quality from what we have known.

Our intellectual and artistic worlds are dominated by the achievements of men and women of genius. Persons of genius often strike us ordinary mortals as at least a little eccentric. We may satisfy our restlessness to account for their special talents by calling them mad. This easy explanation simply substitutes one mystery for another, however, without leading to any deeper understanding.

In my opinion, William Blake was an authentic genius. His achievements were both literary and artistic. He was a remarkable poet and a distinctive painter.

He had very limited recognition on either of these scores during his lifetime. But during the last half century or so his star has risen. Now he is held in the highest esteem by critics, scholars, collectors, and connoisseurs. There is an American Blake Foundation and a Blake Trust, which publishes beautiful color facsimiles of Blake's works (at prices which far exceed what Blake received for the originals). The world of learning has been furnished with a recurrent volume of *Blake Studies,* and with a *Blake Newsletter,* which has been converted into *Blake: An Illustrated Quarterly.* In the last generation, a number of very able scholars have devoted the major part of their intellectual lives to the study of William Blake. What is sometimes called "the Blake Industry" now flourishes mightily.

Many scholars come to the Huntington from all over the world to study Blake. His works are among the most popular subjects in our exhibitions. A section in the Library Exhibition Hall is regularly devoted to his illuminated poetry, manuscript letters, and engravings; his watercolors and other designs are frequently on display in the Art Gallery. Even so, a good many visitors—particularly younger persons—often want to see more Blake.

Research has many thrills. For literary scholars, one of the basic appeals is handling and learning from rare books and manuscripts and visual materials that are by (or closely related to) the writer being studied. These primary sources bring us into what seems like personal contact with our subject, and that contact can sometimes lead to fresh ways of understanding. I would like to try to share this thrill, so far as I can, by communicating material directly from primary sources.

The Huntington Library (which is first of all a place for research) is fortunate to have one of the half-dozen most important Blake collections in the world. This essay is based in large measure on these holdings, which are notable for balance and comprehensiveness. We have eighteen letters written by Blake (more than any other library) and another dozen manuscripts about him; three key books that belonged to him, with his full annotations in their margins; some thirty-three original watercolors by him, ten pencil drawings, two paintings, and his younger brother's sketch book. We have a splendid collection of the hand-illuminated books of Blake's poetry. Blake wrote and etched and colored some sixteen books of his own poetry. There are not many copies of each, for they were all done by hand, mostly when somebody wanted (or was willing) to buy one, and the demand was small. The average number of copies that have been located, after most intensive search, is about a dozen. The Huntington is fortunate to have eleven of these sixteen books—two copies of one of them, and of another the only copy known. The normal way to produce a book, since the time of Gutenberg, is to have it set in type and printed. Only two of Blake's books of poetry were produced in his lifetime in this way. For one of these we have two of some twenty-two known copies; one of ours is a presentation copy signed by Blake, while the other is a presentation copy from John Flaxman, the fellow artist who was responsible for having the book printed. As for the other of the two printed books, we have the only known copy. Finally, we have most of the engravings he made as illustrations for the writings of other persons.

The central issue for Blake is the power of the imagination. It is not easy to see what that power encompassed for him. Nor is it easy to be in tune with his way of looking at the world, or with his way of expressing his thoughts and his feelings. In all of these respects, Blake is the most easily misunderstood person I know about. I hope that we can, in the course of this essay, by coming back again and again to the primary sources, get some true glimpses of the power of the imagination at work in his life and in his poetry.

Does the Eagle know what is in the pit?
Or wilt thou go ask the Mole:
Can Wisdom be put in a silver rod?
Or Love in a golden bowl?

II

Genius can rarely be predicted by the circumstances of birth, and William Blake's background did not promise great things. His father was a small shopkeeper, dealing in haberdashery, and there were no sparks of talent shining openly in his forbears. He was the second of five children in a modest family without many advantages of education or other resources. The only schooling Blake had was in drawing, and he is one of that company of well-educated people, like Alexander Pope and Benjamin Franklin and Mark Twain, who were largely self-taught. It takes a lot of drive and discipline to teach yourself; but it may be the only way for some vigorously independent spirits, of which Blake was certainly one. In his notebook he wrote: "Thank God I never was sent to school/To be Flogd into following the Style of a Fool." Instead, he read voraciously and responsively, with his pen in his hand. In his mature years he learned some Latin, Greek, Italian, and Hebrew on his own. "I go on Merrily with my Greek & Latin," he wrote with jocular expansiveness, and "I read Greek as fluently as an Oxford scholar."

At the age of fourteen, he was apprenticed to an engraver, and he served the usual seven years learning the craft. Before the invention of photography, most engravers earned their living by making illustrations for books. This was to be Blake's lifelong occupation and the principal source of his support. As an engraver, he was a trained professional; in all of his other activities—as a poet and as a painter, specifically—he was a self-taught amateur.

As an apprentice engraver, he was zealous and hardworking. When he had learned the rudiments of his craft, his master set him to the task of copying the work of others. He frequently visited Westminster Abbey to copy monuments on tombs, and the spirit of that place made a profound impression on him. He studied (and copied) prints by the old masters, and he began his own collection of fine prints.

Blake's concept of art—and even of living—was deeply influenced by his trade as an engraver and (in particular) by the work of the Renaissance masters he most admired, Michelangelo, Raphael, and Dürer. His preoccupation with the line—the outline, or the "bounding line" as he called it—derives in part from his early training as an engraver. He wrote:

The great and golden rule of art, as well as of life, is this : That the more distinct, sharp, and wirey the bounding line, the more perfect the work of art ; and the less keen and sharp, the greater is the evidence of weak imitation, plagiarism, and bungling. Great inventors, in all ages, knew this : Protogenes and Apelles knew each other by this line. Rafael and Michael Angelo, and Albert Durer, are known by this and this alone.

What is it that distinguishes· honesty from knavery, but the hard and wirey line of rectitude and certainty in the actions and intentions. Leave out this ln e and you leave out life itself; all is chaos again, and the line of the almighty must be drawn out upon it before man or beast can exist.

In his love of the line, Blake never tired of denouncing artists who seemed to rely first on color and light and shade. "All depends on Form or Outline," Blake wrote. "On where that is put; where that is wrong, the Colouring never can be right; and it is always wrong in Titian and Correggio, Rubens and Rembrandt."

> THE eye that can prefer the Colouring of' Titian and Rubens to that of Michael Angelo and Rafael, ought to be modest and to doubt its own powers.

Genius has the right to be dogmatic, I suppose. Our part as observers of the work of genius is usually less rewarding if we hop into the seat of judgment, more rewarding if we take the role of the inquirer who seeks to understand the fundamental meaning of the dogmatism.

It was during his apprenticeship as an engraver that Blake wrote what turned out to be his first volume of poems. These poems (written between the ages of twelve and twenty) were passed around among friends, and John Flaxman was responsible for arranging to have them printed, under the title *Poetical Sketches*. Here is a passage from one of the relatively conventional poems of Blake's youth, called "To the Evening Star." The poem is in the form of a prayer by a shepherd to the evening star as an angel. It is made up of a series of pictures, or images.

> Let thy weft wind fleep on
> The lake ; fpeak filence with thy glimmering eyes,
> And wafh the dufk with filver. Soon, full foon,
> Doft thou withdraw ; then the wolf rages wide,
> And the lion glares thro' the dun foreft :
> The fleeces'of our flocks are cover'd with
> Thy facred dew : protect them with thine in-
> fluence.

Blake's
visionary
head of
Caractacus

These verses show one of Blake's usual methods of perception, with the focus on the specific and particular. His is not our ordinary way of seeing: "speak silence with thy glimmering eyes,/And wash the dusk with silver." We may not be prepared to think about eyes speaking anything, much less eyes speaking silence. And yet the images make sense despite their odd logic, or perhaps because of it. (Usually we have to try to extend our normal mode of perception in order to take Blake in.) Although the poem portrays a pastoral scene, all is not at peace within it. Inside the world which is this poem, the wolf is raging and the lion is glaring through the dun forest, seeking whom he may devour. Through the major part of Blake's mature writings, the underlying picture is that of a world which has somehow gone wrong because man has misused his natural endowments, a world in need of rebirth and renewal.

Blake's perceptions were often visual, as might be expected of the artist that he was. The eye was, he believed, the basic source of understanding. For the epigraph to his *Visions of the Daughters of Albion*, he wrote:

> The Eye sees more than the Heart knows.

Since he thought that the heart knows a great deal, he intended this statement to make a big claim. "To the Eyes of the Man of Imagination," he wrote to a friend, "Nature is Imagination itself. As a man is, So he Sees."

When Blake finished his apprenticeship as an engraver, at the age of twenty-one, in 1779, he became a student at the Royal Academy. Sir Joshua Reynolds was then president and George Michael Moser was the head of the school. Blake didn't get along with either of them.

When they tried to teach drawing to him, he not only resisted, but he tried to teach them. Here is Blake's own account, recorded as a marginal note in a volume of Reynolds' *Works*, of one encounter with Moser: "I was once looking over the prints from Rafael and Michael Angelo in the Library of the Royal Academy. Moser came to me & said: 'You should not Study these old Hard Stiff & Dry Unfinished Works of Art. Stay a little & I will shew you what you should Study.' He then went & took down Le Bruns & Rubens's Galleries. How I did secretly rage. I also spoke my Mind. . . . I said to Moser, 'These things that you call Finishd are not Even Begun; can they then, be Finishd? The Man who does not know The Beginning, never can know the End of Art.' "

Reynolds didn't come off any better. Blake took some of his designs to Reynolds, and Reynolds suggested that he work with less extravagance and more simplicity, and correct his draftsmanship. Blake did not take the suggestion kindly. Toward Reynolds' theories of art, Blake said he felt "Nothing but Indignation & Resentment." Nevertheless, he studied Reynolds with great care, and his annotations to Reynolds' *Discourses* on art show his close and intelligent understanding of this elegantly traditional view. Blake's own theories of art were not, it now seems, so opposed to those of Reynolds as Blake would have us believe. The basic issues are perhaps Blake's personal dislike of Reynolds and Blake's deep fear (as he expressed it in *Jerusalem*) that "I must Create a System, or be enslav'd by another Mans."

Blake made an early departure from the Royal Academy, and art historians feel that his grasp of the technical details of draftsmanship remained somewhat uncertain throughout his career. Perhaps it seems a pity that Blake could not submit to the discipline of further instruction in art, or that he did not have the chance to study major works of the great masters. The opportunity to study in one of the great centers of Italian art, for example, was not possible for him as a person without money or patronage; even one visit to the Sistine Chapel, to see the frescoes of his favorite Michelangelo, could have been crucial. In England, there were relatively few important paintings on public view and available to him—no great national galleries, for example—and the major source of his knowledge of the art of the past came from his study of black and white engravings. But these are matters for note in understanding what Blake was, not for repining at what he was not.

When Blake left the Royal Academy, he went to work. He set up a print shop, where he made engravings on commission and sold prints. He was also married, at the age of twenty-four, to a young woman of twenty, named Catherine Boucher, whose father's occupation was raising vegetables. Her formal education must have been limited, as she signed the marriage register with an X. Blake taught her to read and write, but apparently he did not go far into grammar. Once when a visitor wondered where the soap was, she is recorded as having replied, "Mr. Blake's skin don't dirt." This remark might in itself provide a good text for an essay on Blake.

It was not that he was thick skinned or insensitive, however; quite the contrary. He tended toward occasional depression, as when he inscribed the stark word "Despair" in his notebook to describe his state of mind. At the age of thirty-six, he scribbled these lines to himself: "I say I shant live five years And if I live one it will be a Wonder"; in fact, he lived thirty-four years more, but he said "I live by Miracle."

He was aware of the fact that he was different from most of the people around him. In a letter to a friend, he scribbled these verses about himself:

115

Blake's visionary
head of Socrates

O why was I born with a different face?
Why was I not born like the rest of my race?
When I look, each one starts! When I speak, I offend;
Then I'm silent & passive & lose every Friend.

Blake's feeling that he was "born with a different face" is a little like Thoreau's comment that "if a man does not keep pace with his companions, perhaps it is because he hears a different drummer. Let him step to the music which he hears," Thoreau wisely concluded, "however measured or far away." The person of genius is often "born with a different face" and "hears a different drummer," and he had better "step to the music which he hears."

Outwardly, the Blakes lived a very quiet life. Although they had no children, they had many devoted friends. In the autograph album of one of them, Blake wrote: "William Blake, one who is very much delighted with being in good company." His friends included a heavy concentration of artists. His contemporaries included John Flaxman, Thomas Stothard, and Henry Fuseli, while George Romney and Sir Thomas Lawrence greatly admired Blake's work. One of Blake's drawings, "The Wise and Foolish Virgins," was Lawrence's favorite among his large collection of drawings. The younger artists who became close friends of Blake included John Linnell, John Varley, Samuel Palmer, Edward Calvert, and George Richmond. All of these artists are so strongly represented in the Huntington collection of drawings, I am happy to say, that we can present as comprehensive an exhibition of the work of the members of Blake's circle as can any other place in the world.

These younger artists called Blake's dwelling "The House of the Interpreter" because—like the House to which they were alluding, in *The Pilgrim's Progress*—it was filled with his interpretations of the world around in the form of drawings and poetry, and in the form of the man himself, whom they found magnetic. In some other ways, the Blake residence was not an impressive house. It consisted of only two rooms: the front room was the sales room for his drawings and engravings; in the other room the Blakes cooked, ate, slept, worked, and received visitors.

Many legends accumulated around the Blakes. The most celebrated, perhaps, is the one about a visit from a friend and patron named Thomas Butts, who found them sitting outdoors in a summerhouse, without any clothes on, reciting passages from *Paradise Lost*, in character. The friend knocked. "Come in!" Blake is supposed to have cried out, "it's only Adam and Eve, you know!" Although the story was told to Blake's biographer by Butts himself, it was hotly disputed for half a century by our Victorian ancestors. We have a manuscript letter from John Linnell to the biographer's

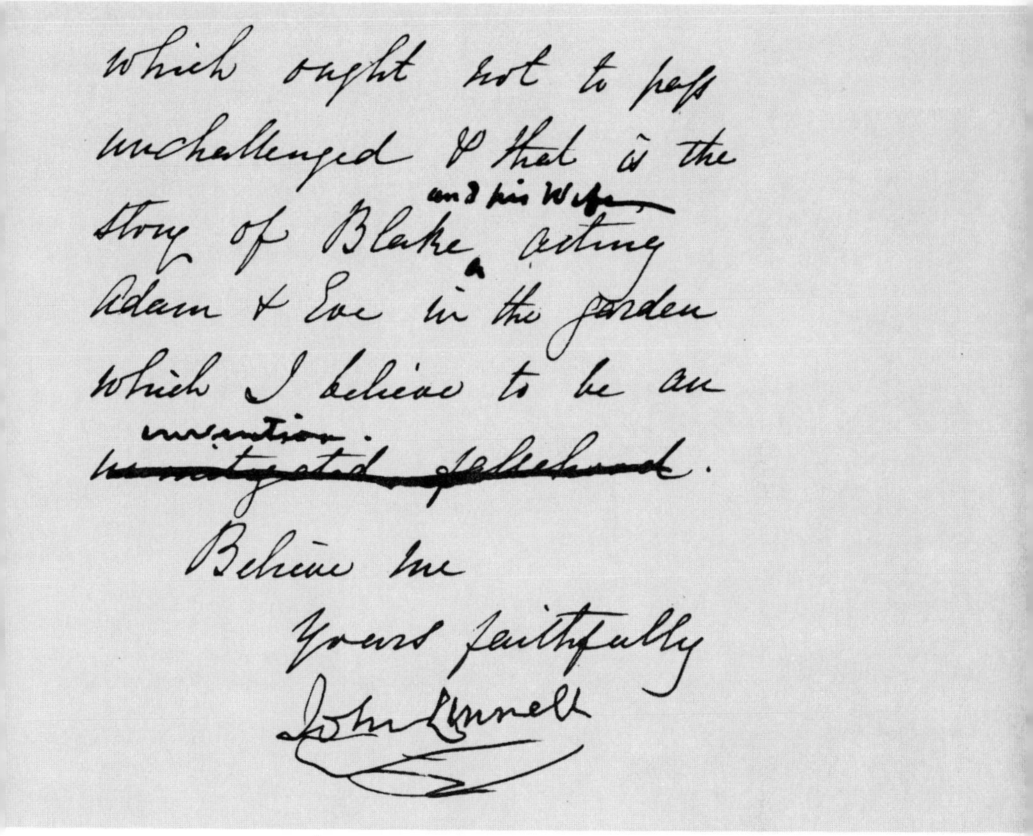

which ought not to pass
unchallenged & that is the
story of Blake and his Wife acting
Adam & Eve in the garden
which I believe to be an
invention ~~unmitigated falsehood~~ .

Believe me

Yours faithfully

John Linnell

widow, written more than fifty years after Blake's death, denouncing the story as "an unmitigated falsehood"; but discretion gained the upper hand, and Linnell carefully lined out the words "unmitigated falsehood" and substituted the word "invention," almost as if he had had the advice of legal counsel. An early biographer tried to save Blake from the ignominy of the Adam and Eve story by saying, "After all, Blake and his wife *were married*." Indeed they were, for forty-five years.

They lived in London throughout their lives except for one period of three years, when a friend named William Hayley offered Blake work as an engraver and painter, with the use of a cottage on his property in the seaside village of Felpham in Sussex. This offer came at what was, financially, a low point in Blake's life. He was delighted at the prospect of going to Felpham; in a manuscript letter in our collection, he addressed Hayley in high spirits as "Leader of My Angels" and said that "My wife is like a flame of many colours of

Leader of My Angels

My Dear & too careful & over joyous Woman has
Exhausted her Strength to Such a degree with expectation &
gladness added to labour in our removal that I fear it
will be Thursday before we can get away from this ———
City I shall not be able to avail myself of the assistance
of Brunos fairies But I Invoke the Good Genii that
Surround Miss Pooles Villa to Shine upon my journey thro
the Petworth road which by your fortunate advice I mean
to take but whether I come on Wednesday or Thursday That
Day shall be marked on my calendar with a Star of the
first magnitude
          Eartham will be my first temple & altar My Wife
is like a flame of many colours of precious jewels whenever she
hears it named Excuse my haste & receive my hearty Love
& Respect
H B Lambeth   I am Dear Sir
Sept 16. 1800   Your Sincere

                        William Blake

My fingers Emit sparks of fire with Expectation of my future labours

precious jewels whenever she hears it named." He added the following postscript: "My fingers Emit sparks of fire with Expectation of my future labours." This show of enthusiasm soon waned, despite the Blakes' best efforts, for Hayley proved to be possessive and directive. He was always telling Blake how to engrave and how to perfect the smallest details of his work. After a year or so of this advice, Blake—remember his spirit of independence—began to squirm. First he wrote epigrams about Hayley in his notebook. Here is one: "Thy Friendship oft has made my heart to ake:/Do be my Enemy for Friendship's sake." Finally, the Blakes gave up and returned to London and to their ordinary, quiet, impoverished life as city dwellers.

Throughout his life, Blake continued his professional career as an engraver. In addition to engraving his own works, he made around 400 plates for commercial book illustrations, in the form of line engravings, etchings, or woodcuts. Often he worked after the designs of other artists, as he did with the illustrations for an edition of Hesiod, thirty-seven plates from designs by John Flaxman. Occasionally, someone else engraved after Blake's designs, as with the illustrations for Blair's *The Grave*, with twelve etchings made by Schiavonetti. Sometimes, Blake both designed and engraved the plates—"invenit & sculpsit" was the expression—as he did with the seven illustrations for Dante or the twenty-two magnificent, revelatory plates for the Book of Job. The commercial illustrations which were his most ambitious were the plates for Young's *Night Thoughts*. Blake spent almost two years on this project, and he made forty-three enormous plates (called "atlas-sized quartos") of engravings which surround the text. Hard work and artistic success were not rewarding financially, however, and the Blakes barely managed to subsist.

In appearance, Blake was a short man, vigorous, with curly red hair and a large head. He and Mrs. Blake were indefatigable walkers, sometimes going as far as forty miles in a day but always ending up at home. Once, when he was sixty-eight, he walked to the coach stop with John Linnell, who was going on a trip. When the coach came, Blake got in with Linnell and they fell to talking while waiting for the scheduled time of departure; but the coach started off without giving notice, and it had gone some distance before Blake was aware of the departure. The rest of the story is contained in a manuscript letter, in our collections, from Blake to Mrs. Linnell: "As I had not paid & did not wish to pay for or take so long a Ride, we with some difficulty made the Coachman understand that one of his Passengers was unwilling to Go, when he obligingly permitted me to get out to my great joy." And of course he walked home.

but as I had not had
& did not wish to pay for or take so long a Ride.. we w[ith]
some difficulty made the Coachman understand that one
of his Passengers was unwilling to Go. when he Obligingly
permitted me to get out to my great joy.

In his last two years, Blake suffered from a series of what he called "shivering fits." (They are thought to have been caused by gallstones and inflammation of the gallbladder, which was the ultimate cause of his death.) In one letter in our collection, written in pencil in a wiggly, barely legible hand, he apologizes for still being in bed at noon after an attack early that morning. "These attacks," he writes, "are too serious at the time to permit me to be out of Bed, but they go off by rest which seems to be All that I want." He encloses the first two engraved plates for the Book of Job and promises to try to be at a meeting the next morning.

A return of the old Shivering fit came on this
Morning as soon as I awaked & I am now in Bed —
Better & as I think almost well If I can possibly
I will be at Mr Lahees tomorrow Morning. these attacks
are too Serious at the time to permit me to be out of
Bed. but they go off by rest which seems to be
All that I want I. I Send the Pilgrims under
your Care with the Two first Plates of Job
    Yours Sincerely Sincerely
        William Blake

12 O Clock
Wednesday

When Falstaff died, he babbled of green fields, if we are to believe the editor who emended the text into sense. Blake died singing. George Richmond described Blake's death, at the age of seventy, to Samuel Palmer: "Just before he died His Countenance became fair. His eyes Brighten'd and He burst out into Singing of the things he saw in Heaven. In truth He Died like a Saint as a person standing by Him Observed."

One of the most touching manuscripts we have is the undertaker's bill for the funeral of William Blake. It is a careful account of fifteen items, beginning with "a 5 foot 9 Elm Coffin covered with black flannel & finished with black varnished Nails, a plate of Inscription, 3 pair handles, lined ruffled & pitched." We also have the handwritten receipt for £10-18-0 which John Linnell paid to discharge the account.

III

So FAR, I have been talking mainly of the externals of Blake's life, but I hope that some sense of the inside shines through. While the events of his life seem ordinary, some of his contemporaries who had never met him thought that he must be mad. Robert Hunt supposed, from having seen some of his pictures and his comments on art, that he was "an unfortunate lunatic, whose personal inoffensiveness secures him from confinement." Some persons were surprised, on first meeting Blake, to discover that he was not a wild madman. If you could yourself have met him, he would probably have seemed neither mad nor ordinary. Let me give you the first impressions of a contemporary, Lady Charlotte Bury, who met him at an evening party at which the painter of "Pinkie," Sir Thomas Lawrence, was also a guest. She confided to her diary that Blake was "not a regular professional painter, but one of those persons who follow the art for its own sweet sake, and derive their happiness from its pursuit. He appeared to me full of beautiful imaginations and genius. . . . He looks care-worn and subdued; but his countenance radiated as he spoke of his favourite pursuit. . . . I could not help contrasting this humble artist with the great and powerful Sir Thomas Lawrence, and thinking that the one was fully if not more worthy of the distinction and the fame to which the other has attained. . . . Every word he uttered spoke the perfect simplicity of his mind, and his total ignorance of all worldly matters."

Parties are usually not the best places to get to know other people in their intellectual and spiritual lives. We have a rare chance to get some insights into Blake's intellectual life, however, by studying his annotations in some of his own books which are now at the Huntington. Blake did not read casually: he devoured and digested books that interested him—even those with which he generally disagreed, like Reynolds' *Discourses.*

One volume that specially intrigued him was Lavater's *Aphorisms on Man,* published in 1788. Blake wrote a lot of aphorisms himself. These, from *The Marriage of Heaven and Hell,* give us some clues about his mind: "The fox condemns the trap, not himself." "You never know what is enough unless you know what is more than enough." "The tygers of wrath are wiser than the horses of instruction." "Prudence is a rich ugly old maid courted by Incapacity."

Lavater suggested that the reader underline, in his book, those aphorisms that affected him agreeably, and set a mark by those that left him uneasy. Blake did both, in about equal measure. He also added comments of his own, from which it is plain that he was a strong, independent, outspoken man.

These comments are primary evidence about Blake, and their reliability is enhanced by their private and personal nature. Popular writers tend to copy one another and often perpetuate the same interpretation, seasoned with a dash of their own skill with language, but scholars learn to go to the primary evidence for the truest enlightenment. Many persons feel that research libraries exist mainly to be scanned for new bits of information. New facts are welcome, of course, but in my opinion the highest role of research libraries is to provide a store of primary evidence that scholars can use as a basis for interpretation and general understanding of larger topics. From studying our primary Blake materials, I have been impressed by the prominence of several of Blake's attitudes that are not altogether apparent from reading the ordinary printed sources. The intensity and unselfconsciousness of Blake's religious feelings, for one thing, and for another, the almost constant play of his comic sense.

In Lavater's *Aphorisms*, Blake underlined number fourteen to show his approval. Lavater had written: "The object of your love is your God." Blake added, "This should be written in gold letters on our temples." The most recurrent comments in Blake's private writings seem to be his religious sentiments. His marginalia in Lavater, for example, are full of such thoughts as these: "Creation is God descending"; "it is the God in *all* that is our companion & friend"; "every thing on earth is the word of God & in its essence is God."

A different kind of aphorism is Lavater's number fifty-four, by which Blake put a big X to express his uneasiness: "Frequent laughing," wrote Lavater, "has been long called a sign of a little mind— whilst the scarcer smile of harmless quiet has been complimented as the mark of a noble heart." Besides expressing his uneasiness, Blake added in the margin, "I hate scarce smiles   I love laughing."

54.
Frequent laughing has been long
[call]ed a fign of a little mind —
[wh]ilft the fcarcer fmile of harmlefs
[qui]et has been complimented as
[the] mark of a noble heart — But
[to] abftain ftom laughing, and ex-
[cit]ing laughter, merely not to of-
[fen]d, or to rifk giving offence,
[is] not to debafe the inward dignity
[of] character — is a power unknown
[to] many a vigorous mind.

*I hate
scarce
smiles
I love
laughing*

Blake's comments on Lavater's
Aphorisms. Left, number 54;
below, number 612.

612.
                    Men carry their character not
Seldom   feldom in their pockets: you might
carry money decide on more than half of your
in my pocket acquaintance, had you will or right
they are gone
really full of to turn their pockets infide out.
paper
                              612.

And so he did, from the gaiety of "Laughing Song" in *Songs of Innocence* to the humor of comical verses. Here is a private example,

Blake's
visionary
head of
Queen Eleanor

from Blake's notebook, that tells a little story:

> I asked a thief to steal me a peach
> He turned up his eyes.
> I ask'd a lithe lady to lie her down
> Holy & meek she cries.
>
> As soon as I went an angel came:
> He wink'd at the thief
> And smil'd at the dame,
> And without one word said
> Had a peach from the tree,
> And still as a maid
> Enjoy'd the lady.

Or, to put Blake's comic sense in another perspective, here is a short passage from one of his letters to a friend, in which he said: "Fun I love, but too much Fun is of all things most loathsom. Mirth is better than Fun, & Happiness is better than Mirth. I feel that a Man may be happy in This World." Certainly Blake was.

Sometimes his sense of comedy took the form of wit, and sometimes of parody. In his copy of a book on the Lord's Prayer, by Dr. Robert John Thornton—now at the Huntington—he filled the margins with objections to the book, which he called "a Most Malignant and Artful attack upon the Kingdom of Jesus." He brought his objections to a head by writing in the flyleaf a version of the Lord's Prayer which he said expressed what this book is really saying about the Lord's Prayer. His parody makes Thornton's book seem ridiculous. "Our Father Augustus Caesar," Blake's parody begins, "who art in these thy Substantial Astronomical Telescopic Heavens, Holiness to thy name or title & reverence to thy shadow, Thy Kingship come upon Earth first & then in Heaven Give us day by day our Real Substantial Money bought Taxed Bread, Deliver from the Holy Ghost . . ." and so forth.

The central part of Blake's life, however, was the world of the imagination, which is the world in which the essential life of the creative artist takes place. "I will not Reason & compare," wrote Blake; "my business is to Create." Creation depended on having visions, through imagination, of what he called (in *Jerusalem*) "the real & eternal World of which this Vegetable Universe is but a faint shadow & in which we shall live in our Eternal or Imaginative Bodies, when these Vegetable Mortal Bodies are no more."

The capacity to have visions of the world of the imagination was, said Blake, a gift of the Holy Spirit.

> I am in Gods presence night & day
> And he never turns his face away.

Blake wrote to a friend that "I see the face of my Heavenly Father; he lays his Hand upon my Head & gives a blessing to all my works; why should I be troubled?" "Every thing that lives is Holy."

Blake felt the power of his imagination growing always stronger. Shortly before he died, he wrote to a friend: "I have been very near the Gates of Death & have returned very weak & an Old Man feeble & tottering, but not in Spirit & Life, not in The Real Man The Imagination which Liveth for Ever. In that I am stronger & stronger as this Foolish Body decays."

Blake's
visionary
head of
Canute

Blake's visions came from his imagination, and he spoke about his visions in a very matter-of-fact way. Often people misunderstood him, however, by taking him in their own vein of literalism. One evening at a party he was describing an interesting scene. "The other evening, taking a walk," said Blake, "I came to a meadow, and at the farther corner of it I saw a fold of lambs. Coming nearer, the ground blushed with flowers; and the wattled cote and its woolly tenants were of an exquisite pastoral beauty. But I looked again, and it proved to be no living flock, but beautiful sculpture." A lady who wanted to take her vacationing children asked him where he had seen this marvelous sight. "*Here*, madam," he replied, touching his forehead.

In Blake's vision, the world looks different from the way we normally see it. In his poem *Jerusalem*, for example, in explaining why the glory of Christianity is that it conquers by forgiveness, tears and sighs and groans become other things:

> For a Tear is an Intellectual thing;
> And a Sigh is the Sword of an Angel King
> And the bitter groan of a Martyrs woe
> Is an Arrow from the Almighties Bow!

IV

Now I WOULD like to see whether several matters of which I have been speaking will fall into place in considering a single poem by Blake. I choose "The Tyger," partly because it is usually on view in our exhibition, partly because it is his best known (but not best understood) short poem.

It was not printed in the ordinary fashion during Blake's life. Charles Lamb speaks about it, in a manuscript letter in our collections, written in 1824 (three years before Blake's death) to a friend who had asked him about Blake. "Blake is a real name, I assure you," wrote Lamb, "and a most extraordinary man, if he be still living."

"His poems have been sold hitherto only in Manuscript. I never read them, but a friend at my desire procured the Sweep Song. There is one to a Tiger, which I have heard recited, beginning

> Tiger Tiger burning bright
> Thro' the desarts of the night—

which is glorious. But alas! I have not the Book, for the man is flown, whither I know not, to Hades, or a Mad House—but I must look on him as one of the most extraordinary persons of the age."

His poems have been sold hitherto only
in Manuscript. I never read them, but a friend at my desire
procured the Sweep Song. There is one to a Tiger, which I have
heard recited, beginning

Tiger Tiger burning bright
Thro' the desarts of the night —

which is glorious. But alas! I have not the Book, for the
man is flown, whither I know not, to Hades, or a Mad House
but I must look on him as one the most extraordinary
persons of the age.

"The Tyger" appears in the *Songs of Experience,* one of the books that Blake etched and colored himself by hand. (All of Blake's poetry that was published during his lifetime was issued in that way, with the two exceptions I have already mentioned.) The method, unlike normal etching, was a complicated one which he developed himself. In essence, it consisted of etching his design and his text onto a copper plate. Then he put the plate on a press and printed it in one ground color. Usually, all of the other colors were then painted in by hand in watercolor, either by Blake or by his wife. Hardly anyone has ever been so completely responsible for his books as Blake was. He was the writer, the designer, the illustrator, the printer, the publisher, and the bookseller. Indeed, he did pretty much everything except make the paper.

The size of the plate on which "The Tyger" appears may seem

surprisingly small. It is not much bigger than a credit card or a driver's license, about 4⅜″ tall and 2¾″ wide. (It has been enlarged a little in both reproductions in this essay as an aid to legibility.) A tiger is stalking across the bottom fourth of the page, away from a big tree, seemingly dead, that runs up and down the right side of the page and shoots its branches across the page between some stanzas. The poem, six little four-line stanzas, occupies the major part of the page.

In Blake's illuminated etchings of verse, the poem and the picture go together, with the visual and the verbal art complementing one another. The result is something like a speaking picture. In order to take in the poem, we have to look carefully at the picture, observing the design and the action, sensing the attitudes and the colors, being aware of the details. Most of us are better trained to deal with words than we are with pictures, and Blake offers a special challenge to our visual senses. The significant developments in Blake studies within the last generation have included a more sophisticated visual understanding of his work.

Blake's imaginary portrait of the head of Socrates, reproduced on page 115, is an example of purely visual interpretation. Blake conveys through this pencil drawing — one of a series of nine of his "visionary heads" at the Huntington — his sense of the character of the subject.

The reproduction of the watercolor painting at the beginning of this essay offers a more complex example for visual interpretation. It tells the story of the conversion of St. Paul, on the road to Damascus, with Jesus appearing to him in the form of a shining light. Blake's interpretation of the event is, of course, wordless: it is what we see that conveys the sense of the glory of Jesus, the majesty of the command, and the awe felt by Saul of Tarsus. Our grasp of it is greater the more we know how to read pictures, the better we remember the narrative, and the more fully we know the iconographical tradition in which this event and its characters were depicted in art.

To return to "The Tyger." The coloring differs somewhat in all the copies I have seen, and this is true for most of Blake's illuminated etchings. Reproductions can give, even at best, only an approximation of Blake's colors, but they reveal something of the differences.

In one of the copies shown, the tree is dull and dark, but there is a spectrum of horizontal bands of color behind the poem, and they may suggest sunset or sunrise. The dark tiger prowls against a light background. This copy was originally owned by Blake's close friend and patron, Thomas Butts, and Blake apparently made and sold it to Butts (for six guineas) in 1806.

In the other copy, the pale yellow background creates an effect somewhat like early morning, and the tiger (lighter in hue than the other one) is walking against a strong blue background. This copy was one of the earliest ones, made by Blake before 1800, once in the collection of Robert Hoe.

The tiger is worth looking at carefully. It may suggest a harmless stuffed toy, but one should keep in mind Blake's proverb that "the tygers of wrath are wiser than the horses of instruction." In fact,

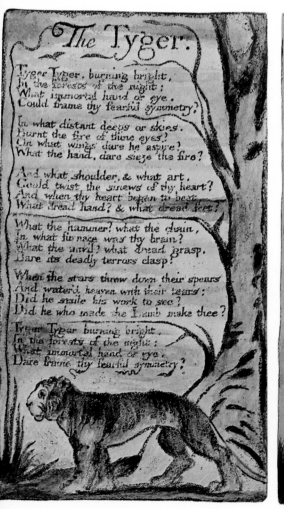
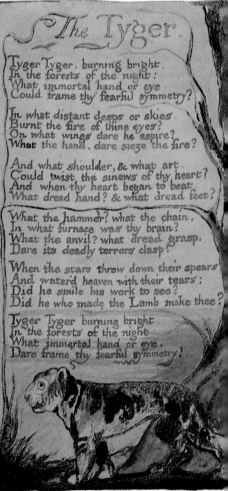

it may be a scary picture if you stare at it long enough in the way that Blake looked. "I can look at a knot in a piece of wood," he said to a friend, "till I am frightened at it."

In a sense, "The Tyger" may be a frightening poem. It is rich and complex, and there are many ways of understanding it. I will offer only a few brief hints about one way of looking at it; there are certainly other possibilities. One background of the poem is the tradition of an Old Testament prophet declaring the forthcoming wrath of God to cleanse and purify the world by fire. Blake also had a strong personal sense that the Second Coming of Christ was at hand, and an apocalyptic expectation pervades much of his writing. Here, in the poem, is the tiger of wrath come according to prophecy. We may fear him because we have come to prefer the material world which we have ourselves created. It is this material world which will be destroyed, and the tiger is a figure of purification as well as of wrath.

The poem is one great question, made up of a multitude of little questions. Who dared to create the tiger? Where he was made? Was the creator pleased with his work? This is our human response to the wrath of God: we might like to squirm away from it, to continue in a fallen state. And so we ask a lot of questions, suggesting that the creation of wrath (or of purification) is not a kindly act and trying to find a way to face the consequences.

Here is the poem. It is best to read it aloud a few times to re-create the music of the verse.

THE TYGER

Tyger Tyger, burning bright,
In the forests of the night:
What immortal hand or eye,
Could frame thy fearful symmetry?

In what distant deeps or skies
Burnt the fire of thine eyes?
On what wings dare he aspire?
What the hand, dare sieze the fire?

And what shoulder, & what art,
Could twist the sinews of thy heart?
And when thy heart began to beat,
What dread hand? & what dread feet?

What the hammer? what the chain,
In what furnace was thy brain?
What the anvil? what dread grasp,
Dare its deadly terrors clasp?

When the stars threw down their spears
And water'd heaven with their tears:
Did he smile his work to see?
Did he who made the Lamb make thee?

Tyger Tyger burning bright,
In the forests of the night:
What immortal hand or eye,
Dare frame thy fearful symmetry?

This poem is, I think, a small masterpiece. As I read the poem, it is a vision of one of the last acts in the history of the world, predicted in the Book of Revelation, of destruction and purification. Thus it fits into the great concept which Blake developed throughout his poetry, that the spiritual world of man is sick because our external world is governed by rationality and mechanization.

"The Tyger" is a vision, the work of Blake's imagination. Imagination turns out to be, for Blake, a way of seeing, a method of perception. Blake's special skill as a poet was his ability to see very deeply. Anyone can learn to see more than he has formerly seen, by developing the power of what Blake called the imagination. The power of that imagination, the power which leads to vision, is, as Blake said, the ability

To see a World in a Grain of Sand
And a Heaven in a Wild Flower
Hold Infinity in the palm of your hand
And Eternity in an hour.

About the illustrations

The *color plates* are all from an original set of the colored engravings made between 1826 and 1838 for *The Birds of America*. They are much reduced in size from the original. These pages (about 6 by 9 inches) have about 1/18 of the area of those original plates, which were made on paper of about 26 by 38 inches. The choice of plates for reproduction has been based in part on their effectiveness in this reduced size. In this essay, the color plates follow the text. Each has a facing page of commentary, mostly in Audubon's own words.

Over. Common Tern. The commentary on this plate is on the last page of this essay.

Above. The portrait of John James Audubon with dog and gun is a popular engraving made in 1861, based on an earlier painting.

Decorations in the borders are details from plates of *The Birds of America*, reproduced without the color of the original and much reduced in size.

Facing page. Part of the engraved title of the original *Birds of America*, much reduced.

THE BIRDS OF AMERICA;

AUDUBON'S *Birds of America* is a beautiful record of the natural world around us. This monumental work occupies one of the five great towers in the Huntington Library exhibition, and it is a visual treat for all of us who go through that hall. The first publication of *The Birds of America* is now about a century and a half in the past, and a reflective and visual review of Audubon and his accomplishments seems appropriate.

First, a short account of the personal history of John James Audubon—what kind of life he lived, how he learned to draw birds so brilliantly, and how his *Birds of America* came to be published. It is a story that would be hard to accept if it were fiction. This review will then conclude with a series of choice plates reproduced in full color from *The Birds of America*. The commentary on each plate, often in the words of Audubon himself, will provide further information on that plate, and on Audubon's outlook on the world of nature and of man.

Audubon is a figure out of myth, and we have endowed him with many attributes, not all of which are strictly true. We call him the father of conservation (a topic in which he was actually not much interested, at least judging by the freedom with which he shot birds); we sentimentalize him (when he was actually quite a rough and ready frontiersman, capable of living with Indians for six weeks at a stretch); and we call him the first important black American artist (when he was actually an altogether white Frenchman who happened to be born in Haiti).

The primary fact is that Audubon was a great naturalist, most of all, one who interpreted birds and animals with deep under-standing of their ways. And he was a great draftsman who portrayed the "feathered tribes" (as he called them) with perhaps finer insight than any other person has ever done.

Audubon was the illegitimate son of a minor French sea captain and an illiterate servant girl. Not a very promising start in life. The girl, Jeanne Rabine, the daughter of a plowman, went out from France in a small merchant ship captained by the senior Audubon. She was intended as a chambermaid for the women-folk of a retired lawyer. Shortly after the arrival in Haiti, Mlle. Rabine moved in with the senior Audubon, who had a house and some land there near Santo Domingo. He also had a Creole housekeeper, who had already borne him two darkish children. Within a few months, Mlle. Rabine was pregnant, she had the son whom we call John James Audubon, and within a few months after his birth she died of fever and infection. This was young Audubon's heritage. And there he lived till he was six years old, when a threat of insurrection by the blacks—a threat that was soon realized, with disemboweling and mutilation of whites—caused his father to return to Haiti, sell his place, and go back to France with his little boy and a younger half-sister, listed as white but really a mulatto.

Home was in western France, near Nantes, in southern Brittany, on the estuary of the Loire River. There the two children joined the childless household of Audubon senior, then forty-six, and his wife Anne, aged sixty. Anne had been a portly, well-to-do widow when they were married twenty years before, and she apparently did not object to her husband's long absences nor to the fruits of those absences. In due course they legally adopted these two children, with the odd result that the natural father became also the adoptive father.

Young Audubon was mainly brought up by his adoptive mother, as his father was away from home a lot, either on business or in his political efforts as a zealous Republican. Young Audubon had arrived in France in 1791, and the years of his childhood were years of violence. The reign of terror came to Nantes with more ruthless repression than almost anywhere else in France. The guillotine was considered too slow, and it was replaced by mass drownings as a way of disposing of enemies of the state.

Young Audubon was an indifferent student. He was, for example, very slack in practicing on his violin; one time his father came home unexpectedly and found the violin not only dusty but also stringless. His father sent him to a military school at the age of twelve to improve his discipline, but after three and a half years the young cadet was dismissed for academic failure. "None but aerial companions," he wrote, "suited my fancy."

He idolized his father and attributed to him his interest in nature. His father "procured birds and flowers for me with great eagerness," wrote Audubon, "—pointed out the elegant movement of the former, the beauty and softness of their plumage, the manifestations of their pleasure or sense of danger,—and the always perfect forms and splendid attire of the latter. My valued preceptor would then speak of the departure and return of birds with the seasons, would describe their haunts, and, more wonderful than all, their change of livery; thus exciting me to study them." He became emotionally involved with birds, and one episode proved traumatic. His adoptive mother had parrots and monkeys in their house. One day a monkey deliberately killed one of the parrots in his view. "My infant heart agonized," he wrote, "at this cruel sight." The incident was "one of the curious things which perhaps led me to love birds, and finally to study them with pleasure infinite."

Study them he did, and tried to draw them. He thought the results were "all stiff, unmeaning profiles," even though (as he said) "many persons praised them to the skies." On his birthdays, he burnt up his collected drawings of the year, knowing that they should be better. His father gave him a book of pictures of birds, and that helped a little. What counted most of all was the encouragement of his father. "My father constantly impressed upon me," he wrote, "that nothing in the world possessing life and animation was easy to imitate, as I would gradually learn. I listened less to others, and more to him; and his kind words and deep interest in my improvement became my law."

When young Audubon reached the age of eighteen, his father decided to send him to America to avoid conscription into Napoleon's forces. So, in 1803, off he went to a farm his father owned, near Philadelphia. He was a handsome young Frenchman, with long, wavy, golden brown hair down to his shoulders, dressed as for a dance with knee breeches and buckled shoes. Soon he got into the swing of life in America and became an avid hunter. Dogs and guns were his constant companions, and he devoted himself more and more to drawing the birds and animals he shot.

He also devoted himself to daily visits to a nearby farm of an Englishman who had a pretty, independent-minded daughter named Lucy Bakewell. Daily, that is, except when her father contrived to have her away on long visits to avoid the romantic, attentive Frenchman, who led her into caves to watch the mating of the pewees (which became so tame that he could take them in his hand and band them).

135

Five years after his arrival, he and Lucy were married, in 1808, when he was twenty-three. For their honeymoon, they set out by stagecoach for the western frontier of Kentucky. When the coach had to climb a long, icy hill, Audubon got out to lighten the load. Lucy stayed inside, and the coach turned over. Although she suffered only minor injuries, the incident made her dread traveling for the rest of her life. And traveling turned out to be one of her husband's major activities, always traveling, traveling in search of birds.

The next fifteen years were spent on the frontier, mainly in Kentucky and Louisiana. Audubon tried many occupations, including managing a lead mill, running a store and a grist mill, painting riverboat interiors, being a taxidermist at the Western Museum in Cincinnati, teaching French and dancing, painting street signs in New Orleans, and drawing portraits for five dollars apiece—enough to keep his family off "the starving list" for a week, he said. He was not very successful in any of his jobs, and in 1819 he was put in jail in Louisville for debts and went bankrupt.

Lucy did not care for the hand-to-mouth existence, especially after their two sons began to grow up. (Their two daughters died in infancy.) When the family got to New Orleans, she took a job as a governess to support the family, and refused to move around, even though her husband threatened divorce if she wouldn't join him. She wouldn't, and fortunately there was no divorce.

Audubon became a real frontiersman. Sometimes he wandered for months at a time. He described himself as looking "just like one of the poorer class of Indians. My beard covered my neck in front, my hair fell much lower at my back, the leather dress which I wore had for months stood in need of repair. To every one I must have seemed immersed in the depths of poverty, perhaps of despair." It was in such a fashion that he watched Daniel Boone kill squirrels at fifty paces by concussion, by hitting the bark beneath them. He listened to Boone's tales of capture by Indians and of escaping by burning his restraining cords at the fire after the Indians had drunk his whiskey. Audubon himself enjoyed frontier humor, as with the traveler who mistook a skunk for a squirrel. "Mr. Audubon, is not that a beautiful squirrel?" "Yes," I answered, "and of a kind that will suffer you to approach it and lay hold of it, if you are well gloved." (The traveler was drenched by the skunk, and Audubon laughed heartily.) Audubon ran many risks on the frontier. Once he got caught in quicksand while trying to recover a great horned owl that he had shot, and he was saved by boatmen with oars and driftwood only when the quicksand was over his armpits. His life was threatened by a runaway slave, and he narrowly escaped drowning while on a duck-hunting expedition. He fell in with the frontier "regulators," and took a hand in meting out rough justice to malefactors, in such a manner as whipping them or burning their cabins.

Throughout his mature life, Audubon considered himself an American. He became a United States citizen in 1812—when he was twenty-seven—but he always continued to talk (and even look) like a Frenchman. A man who met him at a small inn in western Pennsylvania left a vivid account of his speech. The man first saw Audubon in the breakfast room and described him as "an odd fish. He was sitting at a table, before the fire, with a Madras handkerchief wound around his head, exactly in the style of the French mariners, or laborers, in a seaport town. I stepped up to him, and accosted him politely with the words, 'I hope I don't incommode you, by coming to take my breakfast with you.' 'Oh no, sir,' he replied with a strong French accent, that made it sound like 'No, sare.' 'Ah,' I continued, 'you are a Frenchman, sir?' 'No, sare,' he answered, 'hi emm an Heenglishman.' 'Why,' I asked, in return, 'how do you make that out? You look like a Frenchman, and you speak like one.' 'Hi emm an Eenglishman, becas hi got a Heenglish wife,' he answered."

Whatever his accent, the principal object of all his rambling around was the search for birds. Of a month in the neighborhood of Pittsburgh, he said: "I scoured the country for birds." His first objective was to observe birds in their native habitat, to see their behavior, their ways of standing, walking, flying, their feeding and nesting habits, seasonal plumage, and all the rest. He felt that he had to know the birds before he could draw them. He was in the field by daybreak, and he kept at it as long as the birds were around. He traveled up and down the Mississippi and Ohio river areas, and up and down the Atlantic seaboard from Maine to Key West. He spent a winter near Charleston, South Carolina. One summer he hired a boat and crew (at a cost of $2,000) and traveled to Labrador, Newfoundland, and Nova Scotia, bringing back twenty-three large drawings of birds. He availed himself of contacts with the secretary of the treasury and the secretary of the navy to travel on government vessels, and went around the Gulf of Mexico to visit the area we call Texas.

His commitment to drawing birds came very nearly being the obsession that Lucy considered it. His goal was nothing less than to draw every American bird from nature. In the course of years, his representational skill greatly improved. He went from outlines to pencil sketches. He tried drawing from sight and from memory; he used models that he made himself of wood, cork, and wires; he inserted thin wires through the bodies, wings, and legs of newly-killed birds so that he could pose them in a variety of positions. For his medium, he gradually discovered that watercolor was best, though he sometimes added pastel over the watercolor (as in making down feathers), and he sometimes used ink, oil, or egg white for special effects, as for the eye or beak.

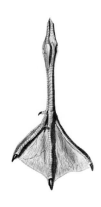

Audubon's progress was beset by a multitude of difficulties, in addition to poverty. The worst were those that endangered his collection of drawings. Once they were lost for some months, once a small collection was burnt up, and once a large collection was eaten by a pair of rats. He could truly say that "not all the incidents in the life of a student of Nature are agreeable in kind."

Beyond trying to represent all of the birds of America, and to represent them in their natural positions, he wanted to portray each bird in its natural size. Here is his full explanation of his method. "Merely to say, that each object of my Illustrations is of the size of nature, were too vague. Not only is every object, as a whole, of the natural size, but also every portion of each object. The compass aided me in its delineation, regulated and corrected each part. The bill, the feet, the legs, the claws, the very feathers as they project one beyond another, have been accurately measured. The birds, almost all of them, were killed by myself, after I had examined their motions and habits, as much as the case admitted, and were regularly drawn on or near the spot where I procured them. The positions may, perhaps, in some instances, appear *outré*; but such supposed exaggerations can afford subject of criticism only to persons unacquainted with the feathered tribes; for, believe me, nothing can be more transient or varied than the attitudes or positions of birds."

Audubon conceived the idea of reproducing and publishing all of his drawings under the title of *The Birds of America*. The only practical way to reproduce them, at that time, was to have them engraved and colored by hand. It would not have been worthwhile to approach any commercial publisher with an idea for a book that would be so big, so expensive, and so difficult to produce. So Audubon decided to publish it himself, by subscription. That is, he himself engaged and paid an engraver to do the work, and he himself sold the books by getting people to agree in advance to take the parts as they were issued.

Since no suitable engraver could be found in the United States, in 1826 Audubon took his precious drawings—240, as many as he had then completed—to Britain. He engaged an engraver in Edinburgh, W. H. Lizars, who did the first ten plates in 1826-27; then a strike of his colorists caused Lizars to give up the job. Audubon then employed Robert Havell, Jr., in London, and Havell touched up the initial ten plates and did all the rest. The job was finally completed in June 1838, nearly twelve years after its beginning.

Large copper plates—many of which are still extant—were used for the engraving. The work was all done by hand, of course. After the engraving of the plate had been completed, then some 200 copies were run off, and these were colored by hand, with watercolor. Havell had as many as fifty men and women working at a time on this project alone. It was demanding work, and it required very close supervision, both by Havell and by Audubon or his son Victor.

Audubon was very exacting, and he threatened and cajoled the engraver to make the work perfect. "Do let me urge you more than ever," he wrote Havell, "to pay the strickest attention to the Colourers for it is doubtless through their evident carelessness that the Work suffers so much at present." Again, "I saw this day several plates of the Baltimore Oriole with the hanging nests no more like my drawing than a chimney sweep is to your beautiful wife." In fact, the differences are slight. The work is remarkably uniform, and the engravings are close to the original drawings.

When the engraving got underway, Audubon had no subscribers at all. He planned to issue the engravings to the subscribers in sets of five, for which he would be paid two guineas. Then each one hundred engravings was to be bound up into a massive folio volume, a size that is called a double elephant folio. There turned out to be 435 plates, and their binding required four huge volumes, each weighing about forty-six pounds and measuring over two and a half feet wide and about three and a half feet tall. These are the consequences of representing all the birds of America in their natural size. The approximate total cost to each subscriber was $1,000—a very substantial sum of money in the 1830s.

Audubon had exceeding difficulty in getting subscribers—and in keeping them. He was on the go most of the time, with a sample portfolio under his arm, trying to sign people up. He went to England with letters of recommendation from Henry Clay, General Andrew Jackson, and others. Audubon was not a timid man, and he met a lot of famous people in England, including the painter of "Pinkie"—as he said, "that eminent and amiable painter, Sir Thomas Lawrence, through a kindred spirit, Thomas Sully of Philadelphia."

He carried a letter of introduction to Lord Rothschild, and he searched out that enormously wealthy London banker in his office. "We walked into his private office without any hindrance," recalled Audubon. "Soon a corpulent man appeared. His face red from the exertion of walking, he hitched his trousers and without noticing anyone draped his fat body into a comfortable chair, clearly caring for no one in this wide world but himself. I stepped forward and with a bow tendered my credentials. 'This,' he said, 'is only a letter of introduction, and from its contents I expect you are the publisher of some book or other, and need my subscription?' In reply to his offensive tone I said I should be *honored* by his subscription to *The Birds of America*. 'I never, Sir, sign my name to any subscription list,' he said. 'But you may send in your work and I will pay for a copy of it. Gentlemen, I am busy—I wish you good morning,' " The parts then out were sent to Lord Rothschild, but when a bill for £100 reached him, Rothschild offered £5 and sent them all back. (Later he relented and subscribed.)

Often, and with reason, Audubon became discouraged. About a selling trip to Oxford, he wrote: "There are here twenty-two colleges intended to promote science in all its branches; I have brought here samples of a work acknowledged to be at least good, and not one of the colleges subscribed. I have been hospitably treated, but with so little encouragement for my work there is no reason for me to remain."

He did sell four sets at Cambridge University, and (at last) two at Oxford. In the United States, the Library of Congress and the State Department subscribed, and so did Harvard, Columbia, and Daniel Webster. He worked up to a total of 308 subscribers, mainly by persuading a multitude of people whose names are not now familiar, such as seven individuals in Savannah, Georgia, and three small libraries in Charleston, South Carolina. The times were hard in the United States in the 1830s, with a chaotic

financial condition, a serious depression, and a panic. Some subscribers discontinued and some died. When the last section was published, he had only 161 subscribers. And he prepared no more than ten or fifteen extra sets. Hence the total number of complete sets of engraved plates was about 175.

He kept careful record of his payments to the engraver. Audubon reckoned his costs, in all, as $115,640. And he prudently added, "Not calculating any of my expense, or that of my family for upwards 14 years." If you count those expenses, he may have lost money on the venture. He was confident that, in fifty years, the work would command "immense prices." He was right about the "immense prices," but, instead of fifty, it took almost 150 years.

Remember that the original cost to subscribers was $1,000 a set. We acquired our set—a fine one, in excellent condition—in 1917 for $3,500, about the going price at that time. But in 1969 a set sold for $216,000, and in 1977 one brought $396,000. I would call those "immense prices."

There have been some good bargains for individual plates. The Long-billed Curlew (with a view of Charleston in the background) was sold by Goodspeed's of Boston in 1905 for $20, in 1929 for $150; Macy's sold that plate in 1931 for $104 and in 1935 for $204. Now, individual plates generally range from about $400 to $1,000 or more. The best bargains in the last fifty years were in 1931, when Macy's broke up four sets and sold the individual plates. You could have then bought the Louisiana Water Thrush for $4.96, or your choice of many plates of warblers for the same modest amount; the Baltimore Oriole was offered for $24.89, the Song Sparrow or the Goldfinch for $14.89, and the Wild Turkey (the most expensive of all) for $224. (The Wild Turkey plate is specially prized, perhaps because it appears first in *The Birds of America*; there are many lovers of the turkey, however, including Benjamin Franklin, who wished that it had been chosen as our national symbol rather than the eagle, which he objected to as "a bird of bad moral character.")

The locations of 134 complete sets of *The Birds of America* are now recorded. And we know, also, that twenty-four sets have been broken up, ten sets were destroyed by fire or in war, and thirteen sets are incomplete. Virtually all of the sets are thus accounted for, in one way or another. And this is not surprising, in view of their size, value, and beauty. No one is likely to mislay a volume, or put it out for the trashman. Of the 134 complete

sets, ninety-four are in the United States, though only about five are west of the Mississippi.

Audubon was incredibly energetic and industrious. During the twelve years while *The Birds of America* was being engraved, he traveled around England and the United States in search of subscribers, he organized trips to see birds, and he painted about half of the birds that were engraved. In addition, he also wrote and published a great five-volume book which he called his *Ornithological Biography*, which was issued between 1831 and 1838. It is a biography of birds, essentially his commentary on the plates of *The Birds of America*, together with anecdotes about his acquaintances, his travels, and his experiences. He had help from a Scotsman, William McGillivray, who supplied the short scientific descriptions and (along with Lucy) revised the rather rough prose of his commentary.

After *The Birds of America*, Audubon embarked on yet another ambitious venture of painting all the four-footed animals in North America and writing a commentary on each of them. He made a strong start, completing half of the 155 plates in *The Quadrupeds of North America*; but it had to be left to his sons to finish the plates and to publish the three folio volumes. Audubon had a stroke in 1847; he became senile, and he died in 1851.

But he left a great treasure behind him in the form of *The Birds of America*. They continue to appeal for a variety of reasons. Because of their beauty of design, arrangement, and color. Because they represent, in a natural setting, living creatures of which we are generally fond. Because they arouse our sympathy for the birds, which usually appear as heroes whenever there is dramatic action. And because they lead us to a deeper understanding of the world around us.

In reading Audubon's comments on the plates, it is clear that his interest was always in the nature, the behavior, and the habits of the birds. He felt that he could not portray the appearance without knowing the reality inside. He was always searching to learn that truth, and the search gave him contentment. "Could I renew the lease of my life," he wrote, "I could not desire to spend it in any other pursuit than that which has at last enabled me to lay before you an account of the habits of our birds."

*Plates
and
Commentaries*

The White-throated Sparrow

This graceful engraving of the White-throated Sparrow features the beauty of poise, of sparseness, of understatement. The drawing, with an adult male sparrow below and a young female above, was made in March, 1822 in Natchez, Mississippi. This plate was one of the first ten engravings for *The Birds of America*. It was originally engraved in Edinburgh by William H. Lizars, then retouched by Robert Havell, Jr. in London before publication.

White-throated sparrows "form groups," wrote Audubon, "sometimes containing from thirty to fifty individuals, and live together in harmony. There is much plaintive softness in their note, which I wish, kind reader, I could describe to you; but this is impossible, although it is yet ringing in my ear, as if I were in those very fields where I have so often listened to it with delight."

"The Dog-wood, of which I have represented a twig in early spring, is a small tree found nearly throughout the Union, but generally preferring such lands as with us are called of second quality, although it occasionally makes its appearance in the richest alluvial deposits."

"Should you, good-natured reader, be a botanist, I hope you will find pleasure while looking at the flowers, the herbs, the shrubs, and the trees, which I have represented; the more so, I imagine, if you have seen them in their native woods."

White Throated Sparrow
FRINGILLA PENSYLVANICA.
1. Male 2. Female
Plant Cornus Florida — Vulgo DogWood.

from Nature by John J.Audubon. F.R.S.E.M.W.S

Printed & Coloured by R.Havell Senr.

Engraved by W.H.Lizars Edinr

The Bluebird

This picture of Bluebirds conveys an astonishing sense of action, with virtually no support from the background. The bird at the top that seems to be flying away is a male; the one at the lower left is a female, feeding a juicy worm to the eager young one; the flower buds are stems of a mullein or flannel plant. The lower pair were drawn about 1820, and Audubon added the male a couple of years later in Louisiana.

"This lovely bird is found in all parts of the United States, where it is generally a permanent resident. It adds to the delight imparted by spring, and enlivens the dull days of winter. Full of innocent vivacity, warbling its ever pleasing notes, and familiar as any bird can be in its natural freedom, it is one of the most agreeable of our feathered favourites. The pure azure of its mantle, and the beautiful glow of its breast, render it conspicuous, as it flits through the orchards and gardens, crosses the fields or meadows, or hops along by the road-side. Its visits are always welcomed by those who know it best."

"When March returns, the male commences his courtship, manifesting as much tenderness and affection towards his chosen one, as the dove itself. Martins and House-wrens! be prepared to encounter his anger, or keep at a respectful distance. Even the wily cat he will torment with querulous chirpings, whenever he sees her in the path from which he wishes to pick up an insect for his mate."

Blue-bird.

SYLVIA SIALIS,

Male 1. Female 2. Young 3.
Great Mullein Verbascum Thapsus.

The Pine Siskin

This graceful plate features a pair of Pine Siskins (or Pine Finches), perched on a branch of black larch, busily eating. Audubon often made a pleasing pattern out of an odd, even awkward arrangement that depicted normal habits of the birds.

Audubon observed these birds in 1832 in Canada, in New Brunswick. He wrote that he "frequently met with flocks of these birds feeding amid the branches of the tallest fir trees, as well as on the seeds of the thistles of that country, much in the manner of the American Goldfinch, and the European Siskin. When disturbed, they would rise high in the air in an irregular flight, emitting their peculiar call-note as they flew; but would always realight as soon as another group of thistles was seen by them. When feeding, they often hung head downwards like so many Titmice, and as often would balance themselves on the wing, as if afraid to alight on the sharp points of the plants, which after all they appeared greatly to prefer to all others."

Pine Finch.
FRINGILLA PINUS.
Male 1. Female, 2.
Pinus pendula. Black Larch.

Nature by J.J.Audubon, F.R.S. F.L.S.

Engraved, Printed, & Coloured, by R. Havell, 1835.

The Field Sparrow

This single male Field Sparrow seems to be the centerpiece of a natural arrangement, and so it was in actuality. "Travelling from Great Egg Harbour" in New Jersey in 1829, wrote Audubon, "towards Philadelphia, I found a nest of this species placed at the foot of a bush growing in almost pure sand. Near it were the plants which you see accompanying the figure." The flower is a form of wild orchid (*Calopogon tuberous*), and the bush is a blueberry.

"This diminutive and elegant species of Finch is a social and peaceable bird. When the breeding season is at hand they disperse, move off in pairs, and throw themselves into old pasture grounds, overgrown with low bushes, on the tops of which the males may be heard practising their vocal powers. They usually breed on the ground, at the foot of a small bush or rank-weed; but I have also found several of their nests on the lower branches of trees, a foot or two from the ground. So prolific is this species, that I have observed a pair raise three broods in one summer, the amount of individuals produced being fifteen. The young run after their parents, leaving the nest before they can fly, and are left to shift for themselves ere they are fully fledged; but as they can find every where abundance of insects, berries, and small seeds, they contrive to get on without help."

Field Sparrow FRINGILLA PUSILLA, *Will.*
Male. *Calopogon pulchellum.* & *Vaccinium tenellum.*

Drawn by J. J. Audubon, F.R.S. F.L.S.

Engraved, Printed & Coloured by R. Havell, London, 1832.

Anna's Hummingbird

These Hummingbirds, the most common variety in Southern California, are around a stalk of pink hibiscus. Audubon drew the female and her nest at the bottom from specimens sent him in England by a friend in the Rocky Mountains, and he used specimens from an English collection for the four males above. The hibiscus was added by an assistant, Maria Martin; five different people (including his two sons) occasionally assisted him in this way, and the articulation of their work with his seems almost miraculous.

"My good friend Thomas Nuttall, while travelling from the Rocky Mountains toward California, happened to observe on a low oak bush a Humming Bird's nest on which the female was sitting. Having cautiously approached, he secured the bird with his hat. The male in the mean time fluttered angrily around, but as my friend had not a gun, he was unable to procure it."

"The nest, which he has presented to me, is attached to a small branch, and several leaves from a twig issuing from it, which have apparently been bent down for the purpose. It is very small, even for the size of the bird, being an inch and a half in depth, and an inch and a quarter in breadth externally at the mouth, while its internal diameter is ten-twelfths, and its depth eight and a half twelfths. It is of a conical form, and composed of the cottony down apparently of some species of willow, intermixed with scales of catkins and a few feathers, and lined with the same substances. The eggs, two in number, are pure white, of a nearly elliptical form, five-twelfths of an inch long, and three and a quarter twelfths in their greatest breadth."

Columbian Humming Bird,
TROCHILUS ANNA, *Leason.*
1.♂.3.♂ Male. 5 Female and Nest.
Plant. Hibiscus Virginicus.

Drawn by J. J. Audubon, F.R.S. F.L.S.   Engraved Printed and Coloured by Rob.ᵗ Havell, 1828.

The Goldfinch

This pair of Goldfinches is looking for seeds and insects on a thistle plant. The male is above and the female below. Audubon made the painting in New York state in about 1824; it was engraved in 1828.

"In ascending along the shores of the Mohawk river, in the month of August, I have met more of these pretty birds in the course of a day's walk than anywhere else; and whenever a thistle was to be seen along either bank of the New York Canal, it was ornamented with one or more Goldfinches. They tear up the down and withered petals of the ripening flowers with ease, leaning downwards upon them, eat off the seed, and allow the down to float in the air. The remarkable plumage of the male, as well as its song, are at this season very agreeable; and so familiar are these birds, that they suffer you to approach within a few yards, before they leave the plant on which they are seated."

"So fond of each other's company are they, that a party of them passing on the wing will alter its course at the calling of a single one perched on a tree. This call is uttered with much emphasis: the bird prolongs its usual note, without much alteration, and as the party approaches, erects its body, and moves it to the right and left, as if turning on a pivot, apparently pleased at shewing the beauty of its plumage and the elegance of its manners. No sooner has the flock, previously on wing, alighted, than the whole party plume themselves, and then perform a little sweet concert."

llow Bird or American Goldfinch.
Male 1. F 2.
CARDUELIS AMERICANA.
nt Cnicus lanceolatus, Vulgo Common Thistle.

om Nature and Published by John J. Audubon, F.R.S.E. F.L.S. M.W.S. Engraved, Printed & Coloured by R. Havell & Son. London . 18

The Flicker

Here is a whole plate of Flickers (or Golden-winged Wood-peckers). The two quarreling at the top (with one showing off the yellow-gold underfeathers) are females. The other three, all males, are attending to male business of eating a worm, hiding behind the tree, and (out on the little branch) looking thoughtful.

Audubon said of these flickers that "it is generally agreeable to be in the company of individuals who are naturally animated and pleasant. For this reason, nothing can be more gratifying than the society of Woodpeckers in the forests."

"The flight of this species is strong and prolonged, being per-formed in a straighter manner than that of any other of our Woodpeckers. They propel themselves by numerous beats of the wings, with short intervals of sailing, during which they scarcely fall from the horizontal. When passing from one tree to another on wing, they also fly in a straight line, until within a few yards of the spot on which they intend to alight, when they suddenly raise themselves a few feet, and fasten themselves to the bark of the trunk by their claws and tail. No sooner has the bird alighted, if it be not pursued or have suspicions of any object about it, than it immediately nods its head, and utters its well-known note 'Flicker.' "

PLATE 37.

Gold-winged Woodpecker, Male 1 Fd.

PICUS AURATUS.

The Baltimore Oriole

These Baltimore Orioles are shown around their nest, which is hanging from the branch of a tulip tree in bloom. Audubon was delighted by their beauty and astonished by their cleverness in designing and building their nests to suit the climate and the location.

In Louisiana, they use Spanish moss, observed Audubon, and create an air-conditioned effect. The male "flies to the ground, searches for the longest and driest filaments of the moss, which in that State is known by the name of Spanish Beard, and whenever he finds one fit for his purpose, ascends to the favourite spot where the nest is to be, uttering all the while a continued chirrup, which seems to imply that he knows no fear, but on the contrary fancies himself the acknowledged king of the woods. This sort of chirruping becomes louder, and is emitted in an angry tone, whenever an enemy approaches, or the bird is accidentally surprised, the sight of a cat or a dog being always likely to produce it. No sooner does he reach the branches, than with bill and claws, aided by an astonishing sagacity, he fastens one end of the moss to a twig, with as much art as a sailor might do, and takes up the other end, which he secures also, but to another twig a few inches off, leaving the thread floating in the air like a swing, the curve of which is perhaps seven or eight inches from the twigs. The female comes to his assistance with another filament of moss, or perhaps some cotton thread, or other fibrous substance, inspects the work which her mate has done, and immediately commences her operations, placing each thread in a contrary direction to those arranged by her lordly mate, and making the whole cross and recross, so as to form an irregular net-work. Their love increases daily as they see the graceful fabric approaching perfection, until their conjugal affection and faith become as complete as in any species of birds with which I am acquainted."

"The nest has now been woven from the bottom to the top, and so secured that no tempest can carry it off without breaking the branch to which it is suspended."

Drawn from Nature by J.J. Audubon. F.R.S.E. M.W.S.

Baltimore Oriole.
ICTERUS BALTIMORE.
Plant Vulgo. Yellow Poplar.
Liriodendron Tulipifera.

Engraved by R. Havell, Jun.

The Snowy Egret

This Snowy Egret (or Heron) is presiding over the scene of a rice plantation near Charleston, South Carolina, where Audubon spent the spring of 1832. The perspective makes it seem that we share this magnificent bird's outlook on the world of a plantation with barns, a pond, and a man working in the field. (The landscape was added by George Lehman, Audubon's assistant.)

"At the approach of autumn, the crest assumes a form, and the feathers of the lower parts of the neck in front become considerably lengthened, the feet acquire a yellow tint, and the legs are marked with black on a yellowish ground; but the flowing feathers of the back do not appear until the approach of spring, when they grow rapidly, become recurved, and remain until the young are hatched, when they fall off."

"Their motions are generally quick and elegant, and, while pursuing small fishes, they run swiftly through the shallows, throwing up their wings. Twenty or thirty seen at once along the margins of a marsh or a river, while engaged in procuring their food, form a most agreeable sight."

Snowy Heron or White Egret.
ARDEA CANDIDISSIMA,
Male adult Spring plumage.

The Great Horned Owl

These Owls are magnificently portrayed on an impressive plate. They stare you down, with tufted ears that look like horns, perhaps. They may seem scary to those who have anxiety inside, or humorous in their cross-eyed way to those who do not. The minimum background of a dead branch leaves the attention on the owls, with delight in the unfamiliar.

"The flight of the Great Horned Owl is elevated, rapid and graceful. Now and then, it glides silently close over the earth, with incomparable velocity, and drops, as if shot dead, on the prey beneath. At other times, it suddenly alights on the top of a fence-stake or a dead stump, shakes its feathers, arranges them, and utters a skriek so horrid that the woods around echo to its dismal sound. Now, it seems as if you heard the barking of a cur-dog; again, the notes are so rough and mingled together, that they might be mistaken for the last gurglings of a murdered person, striving in vain to call for assistance; at another time, when not more than fifty yards distant, it utters its more usual *hoo, hoo, hoo-e,* in so peculiar an under tone, that a person unacquainted with the notes of this species might easily conceive them to be produced by an Owl more than a mile distant."

Great horned Owl.

Male 1. Female 2.

Strix Virginiana.

y John J. Audubon FRSE FLS MWS.

Engraved by R. Havell Jun.t Printed & Coloured by R. Havell Senr. London 1830.

The Mallard Duck

This handsome plate, depicting two pairs of Mallard Ducks, is an elegant feat of draftsmanship. The female on the right is reaching for a snail, and her drake is cooperating by pulling down the grass. The female on the left is sampling the water, while her drake is simply looking wise and handsome.

The mallard is the forebear of almost all varieties of domesticated ducks. But, wrote Audubon, "how brisk are all his motions compared with those of his brethren that waddle across your poultry-yard! how much more graceful in form and neat in apparel! The duck at home is the descendant of a race of slaves. But the free-born, the untamed duck of the swamps,—see how he springs on wing, and hies away over the woods. Look at that Mallard as he floats on the lake; see his elevated head glittering with emerald-green, his amber eyes glancing in the light! The wary bird draws his feet under his body, springs upon them, opens his wings, and with loud quacks bids you farewell."

The Common Tern
(at the beginning of this essay)

This view of the Tern in flight is an example of breathtaking design. One could meditate a great while over this achievement, as much as Audubon meditated on the "plaintive cry" of the Tern's, whose actions retained for him elements of an unsolvable mystery.

"With an easy and buoyant flight," he wrote, "the Tern visits the whole of our indented coasts, with the intention of procuring food, or of rearing its young, amidst all the comforts and enjoyments which kind Nature has provided for it. Full of agreeable sensations, the mated pair glide along side by side, as gaily as ever glided bridegroom and bride. The air is warm, the sky of the purest azure, and in every nook the glittering fry tempts them to satiate their appetite."

"I have many times seen the Common Tern suddenly fly up and come close over a man or a dog, without the least apparent provocation, indeed when far distant from its nest, and then pass and repass repeatedly within a few yards, emitting a plaintive cry, as if its eggs or young were in the immediate vicinity."

Thoreau's
Walden

About the illustrations

Over. The cabin built by Thoreau at Walden Pond. This engraving, made for the title page of the first edition of *Walden,* was based on a drawing by Thoreau's sister Sophia. Thoreau regretted that the trees looked like firs instead of pines, but the picture is the most authentic portrayal of the cabin.

Above. This engraved portrait shows Thoreau at the age of 44, in 1861, about a year before his death.

Facing page. Thoreau's draft for the title page of *Walden.*

Facsimile quotations in the text are from the first edition of *Walden,* published in 1854.

May Alcott drawings. Three Concord sketches by May Alcott are included in this essay and identified by brief captions. They are from a little-known book of twelve photographs of her drawings; it was published in 1869 under the title *Concord Sketches.* May Alcott (officially Abby May Alcott, 1840-79) was the fourth daughter of Bronson Alcott and the younger sister of Louisa May Alcott. The Alcotts lived in Concord and knew Thoreau well.

Walden,
Life in the Woods.
By
Henry D. Thoreau;

I

THOREAU'S *Walden* occupies a special place in our American heritage. Moreover, the book is still alive and vibrant, and it reaches out to touch the life of each one of us who is receptive. It was not always so. *Walden* made little splash when it first appeared, in 1854. It is only within the last half a century that it has become prominent, within the last generation that it has come to be thought a central document in American experience.

Walden is a great masterpiece which has a special association with the Huntington because the original manuscripts of it are here. It is a book that explores basic questions about the way we live and the way we might live. It is different from most other books, as Thoreau was different from most other men. It is a personal book: about its author, very deeply; but also about its reader, and it means different things to us as we change. It is about the world of nature outside of us, but also about the world of man within us. It is a book to be read with affection born of understanding.

What, may we ask, is the source of its appeal? Go back to the book itself. Go back to Thoreau the man. It is a great advantage to have a large repository of materials to call on. The Huntington Library has some three or four thousand pages of Thoreau manuscripts, for example, as well as a quantity of proof sheets of his writings as he corrected them, many manuscript letters by him, to him, and about him, and a first-class collection of his printed works. I would like to share with you something of what is contained in those rare books and manuscripts.

Thoreau was a poor boy from Concord, Massachusetts. His father was a pencil maker and his mother ran a boardinghouse. Thoreau

Harvard in Thoreau's time. This engraving of the principal buildings was published in 1830; Thoreau entered in 1833 and was graduated in 1837.

managed, however, to go to Harvard College. We have at the Huntington a number of the themes, in manuscript, that he wrote in college, and they tell a lot about him. While I think that most of us share the feeling of not especially wanting anybody to read our academic exercises—in fact, of being dismayed if we thought they were in existence—one does gain a sense of immediacy from handling and reading the papers that Thoreau turned in when he was an undergraduate student. One of those papers, on servile respect for what is foreign, sounds the theme of his lifelong love of nature, along with his dislike for conventional expression. In it, he deplores poets who "are prone to sing of skylarks and nightingales, perched on hedges, to the neglect of the homely robin-red-breast, and the straggling rail-fences of their own native land." Another essay reveals his early sense of independence. In writing on the assigned topic that "we are apt to become what others, (however erroneously) think us to be," Thoreau speaks scornfully of that "false shame which many feel lest they be considered singular or eccentric, and therefore they run into the opposite extreme, become all things to all men, and conform to existing customs and rules, whether good or bad." As we shall see, he had no fear of being considered "singular or eccentric," and he certainly did not "run into the opposite extreme" of conformity.

Thoreau graduated from Harvard in the class of 1837. Richard Henry Dana (author of *Two Years Before the Mast*) was in the same class; Jones Very was in the class ahead, James Russell Lowell in the class behind, and Edward Everett Hale was two classes later. Commencement in 1837 featured what turned out to be the most famous Phi Beta Kappa address of all time: Ralph Waldo Emerson's "The American Scholar," which has been called "our intellectual

Declaration of Independence." But it is not certain that Thoreau—who was to be in the forefront of American intellectual independence—even attended. Harvard, in the routine way, offered him the Master of Arts degree, three years after he graduated. Thoreau declined, however, for there was a graduation fee of $5 payable before you could get the degree, and $5 was a considerable sum of money. Thoreau did spend $5 on some occasions. When Harvard asked him for a contribution for the Library, Thoreau sent $5 and wrote: "I would gladly give you more but this exceeds my income from all sources together for the last four months."

After Harvard, Thoreau had gone back to Concord. Following a short spell of schoolteaching, he became a day laborer. "If a man must have money," he wrote to Horace Greeley, "and he needs but the smallest amount, the true and independent way to earn it is by day-labor with his hands at a dollar a day. . . . There is no reason why the scholar who professes to be a little wiser than the mass of men, should not do his work in the ditch occasionally, and by means of his superior wisdom make much less suffice for him." (This sentiment is probably less appealing to scholars than to day laborers.)

Thoreau worked regularly for Emerson, his fellow townsman, as a handyman. He had a room in the Emerson house—the most noble edifice in Concord, both then and now—and he worked about one day a week in return for room and meals. If he worked extra hours, he got paid real money. I ran across a scrap of paper, among our manuscript collections, on which Thoreau kept one of his accounts. Part of it reads: "surveyed lumber &c half a day; white washing 4 hours; papering 8 hours; papering and white washing

The Emerson house in Concord, where Thoreau lived and worked. This picture is an 1869 photograph of a drawing by May Alcott.

4 hours; budding 2 half days; hoeing 3 hours. . . . Mr. Emerson owes me $5.65."

The Emerson household was rather formal and polite. Mrs. Emerson was sickly and shy to the point of neuroticism: she said that when she had to give an order in the kitchen, she felt like a boy who throws a rock and then quickly runs away lest he be caught. Her first name was Lydia, but her husband insisted that she change it to Lidian, as he thought "Lidian Emerson" had a better ring to it. Emerson was our most distinguished man of letters, and he and Thoreau became fast friends, but perhaps not intimate friends: speaking of their friendship, Emerson wrote in his Journal, "As for taking Thoreau's arm, I should as soon take the arm of an elm tree."

Thoreau also came to know Hawthorne. The Hawthornes invited him to dinner soon after they moved to Concord, and the next day Hawthorne gave an account in his Journal of Thoreau, who was then just barely twenty-five years old. "Mr. Thorow dined with us yesterday." (The spelling may be a clue to the pronunciation of Thoreau's name; most people seemed to put the primary accent on the first syllable.) "He is a singular character—a young man with much of wild original nature still remaining in him; and so far as he is sophisticated, it is in a way and method of his own. He is as ugly as sin, long-nosed, queer-mouthed, and with uncouth and rustic, although courteous manners, corresponding very well with such an exterior. But his ugliness is of an honest and agreeable fashion, and becomes him better than beauty. On the whole, I find him a healthy and wholesome man to know." Actually, Thoreau didn't pride himself on his own looks. To a person who wrote asking him for a photograph, Thoreau answered: "You have the best of me in my books. I am not worth seeing personally—the stuttering, blundering, clodhopper that I am."

Shortly after he finished college, Thoreau began an autobiographical sketch. Although he did not carry it beyond the first paragraph, his view of himself is revealing, as a young man who was to live life in the woods and to write *Walden*. "It may be well," he wrote, "if first of all I should give some account first of my species and variety. I am about five feet 7 inches in height—of a light complexion, rather slimly built, and just approaching the Roman age of manhood. One who faces West oftener than East—walks out of the house with a better grace than he goes in—who loves winter as well as summer—forest as well as field—darkness as well as light. Rather solitary than gregarious—not migratory nor dormant—but to be raised at any season, by day or night, not by the pulling of any bell wire, but by a smart stroke upon any pine tree in the woods of Concord."

Ralph Waldo Emerson describes Thoreau. These passages are from Emerson's own manuscript. The one below describes Thoreau's physical appearance; the one on the next page touches on Thoreau's inner nature. They may be compared with Thoreau's self-description on the preceding page. The engraving of Emerson (right) shows him at about the age of 50.

He was of a short stature, firmly built, of light complexion, with strong, steady blue eye, and a grave aspect, his face covered in the late years with a becoming beard. His senses were acute, his frame wellknit & hard, his eyes keen his hands strong & skilful in the use of tools. And there was a perfect fitness of body & mind. He could pace

He was equally interested in
every natural fact. The
depth of his perception found
likeness of law throughout
nature, & I know not any
genius who so swiftly
inferred universal law
from the single fact. He
was no pedant of a
department. His eye was
open to beauty

II

IT WAS IN 1845, when he was twenty-seven, that Thoreau heeded the call of the pine trees and—walking out of the house "with a better grace"—went to live in the woods near Walden Pond. This was the experience that would form the framework for the book which he entitled "Walden: Or, Life in the Woods." He borrowed an axe and built a cabin on land owned by Emerson. But it is better to read the story as he wrote it himself in *Walden*, because that account is a good introduction to Thoreau the man and to the book:

Near the end of March, 1845, I borrowed an axe and went down to the woods by Walden Pond, nearest to where I intended to build my house, and began to cut down some tall arrowy white pines, still in their youth, for timber. It is difficult to begin without borrowing, but perhaps it is the most generous course thus to permit your fellow-men to have an interest in your enterprise. The owner of the axe, as he released his hold on it, said that it was the apple of his eye; but I returned it sharper than I received it. It was a pleasant hillside where I worked, covered with pine woods, through which I looked out on the pond, and a small open field in the woods where pines and hickories were springing up. The ice in the pond was not yet dissolved, though there were some open spaces, and it was all dark colored and saturated with water. There were some slight flurries of snow during the days that I worked there; but for the most part when I came out on to the railroad, on my way home, its yellow sand heap stretched away gleaming in the hazy atmosphere, and the rails shone in the spring sun, and I heard the lark and pewee and other birds already come to commence another year with us. They were pleasant spring days, in which the winter of man's discontent was thawing as well as the earth, and the life that had lain torpid began to stretch itself.

Thoreau built his cabin, and planted his bean field, and observed the animals and birds and plants through all the seasons of the year. Otherwise, he seemed to be doing nothing at all—since thinking and writing are seemingly nothing. His friends puzzled over this strange behavior. Since his friends kept asking the reason why, he gave his answer right in the text of *Walden*. "I went to the woods," he wrote—and I ask you to observe the cadence of his prose, here, and in all of the passages I quote. It is most rewarding to read them aloud, and listen to the sound of his words. For in the cadence of his prose, in its strength and simplicity and harmony, in his cadence is the essence of his meaning. Thoreau should be listened to, and what strikes your ear is a clue to what *Walden* is all about. "I went to the woods," he wrote,

> because I wished to live deliberately, to front only the essential facts of life, and see if I could not learn what it had to teach, and not, when I came to die, discover that I had not lived. I did not wish to live what was not life, living is so dear; nor did I wish to practise resignation, unless it was quite necessary. I wanted to live deep and suck out all the marrow of life, to live so sturdily and Spartan-like as to put to rout all that was not life

Thoreau stayed in his cabin two years and two months and two days. Neither rain nor snow deterred him from his appointed rounds. "I frequently tramped," he wrote, "eight or ten miles through the deepest snow to keep an appointment with a beech-tree, or a yellow-birch, or an old acquaintance among the pines."

"To keep an appointment with a beech-tree." A thread of quiet wit or irony runs through Thoreau's writing, drawing it all together into one garment, and the right reaction to many passages is a smile, or even a chuckle. "For many years," he writes, with mock solemnity, "I was self-appointed inspector of snow storms and rain storms, and did my duty faithfully." Sometimes his sense of fun is a little more sardonic. As, when writing about fashions, he says, "The head monkey at Paris puts on a traveller's cap, and all the monkeys in America do the same." Or, when talking about the building of the telegraph, he writes: "We are in great haste to construct a magnetic telegraph from Maine to Texas; but Maine and Texas, it may be, have nothing important to communicate." In fact, Thoreau was not much interested in what we call news. "Blessed are they who never read a newspaper," he wrote to a friend, "for they shall see Nature, and through her, God."

One of the great themes in *Walden* is the love of nature. I ran across a nice symbolic example of nature winning out over civilization in one of our detached manuscripts. We have the summons that Thoreau received to go to court as an expert witness in a civil case, the summons sourly concluding, "Hereof fail not, As you will answer your default under the pains and penalty in the law in that behalf made and provided." But after he had duly appeared in court, Thoreau kept the summons and he filled the entire back of it with such notes as these: "Tortoises drop into brook Mar 30. Pewee & lark heard 30 Mar. A robin sings at eve 1st Ap. Earth has a greenish tinge. Elms generally in bloom." And so on and so forth, with the pewees and the robins having the last word over the legal case. Thoreau had the habit of recording everything he could on whatever scrap of paper came to hand. His greatest concern, perhaps, was to set down the details of his observations about the world of nature.

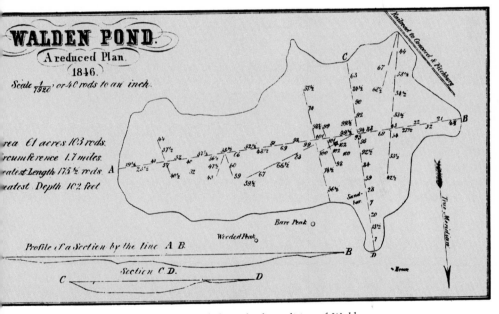

This surveyor's drawing of Walden Pond, from the first edition of *Walden*, was made by Thoreau himself. "As I was desirous to recover the long lost bottom of Walden Pond, I surveyed it carefully, before the ice broke up, early in '46, with compass and chain and sounding line."

Emerson took a kind of standard parental attitude toward Thoreau's preoccupation with nature. He confided in his Journal that "Thoreau wants a little ambition in his mixture. Fault of this, instead of being the head of American Engineers, he is captain of a huckle-

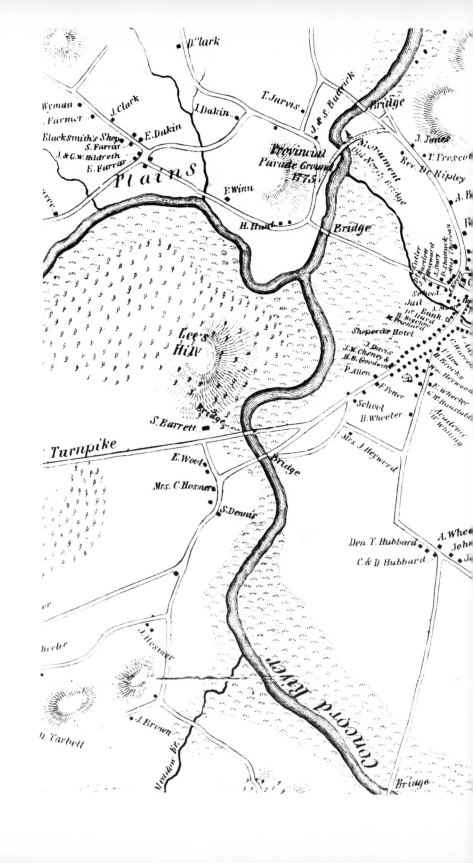

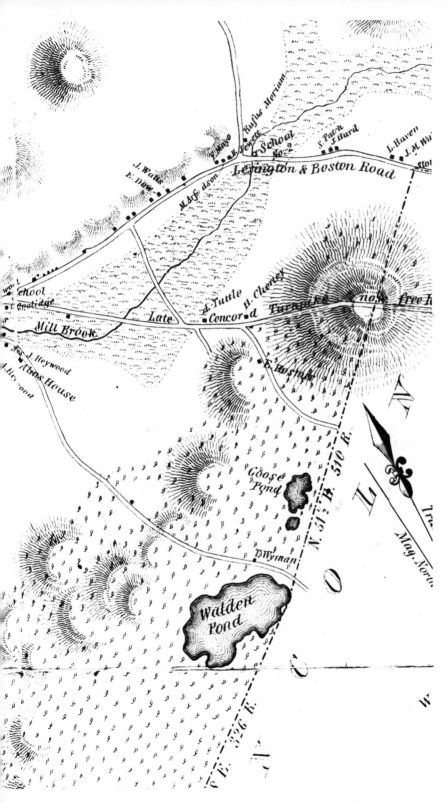

The Concord-Walden Pond area in 1830. This map served as the frontispiece for
[S]emuel Shattuck's bicentennial history of Concord, published in 1835. Various
[l]andmarks, such as the jail, are identified.

berry party." Mothers and fathers would like to see promising children use their talents, and not waste themselves as Thoreau seemed to be doing. Hawthorne admired Thoreau's "great qualities of intellect and character" but thought him "a wild, irregular, Indian-like sort of fellow, who can find no occupation in life that suits him."

For a while, Thoreau himself had misgivings about not using his education in a gainful occupation. "Wading in retired meadows," he wrote, "in sloughs and bog-holes, in forlorn and savage places, appeared for an instant trivial to me who had been sent to school and college; but as I ran down the hill toward the reddening west, with the rainbow over my shoulder, and some faint tinkling sounds borne to my ear through the cleansed air," the misgivings disappeared. "Let not to get a living be thy trade," he thought, "but thy sport."

Thoreau came to look on the life of one human being as transitory, and even mankind as transient. Nature was permanent. After telling about the former inhabitants around Walden Pond and the houses they built there, Thoreau said—and notice again his rhythms, as well as his loving recital of the names of growing things:

> Now only a dent in the earth marks the site of these dwellings, with buried cellar stones, and strawberries, raspberries, thimble-berries, hazel-bushes, and sumachs growing in the sunny sward there; some pitch-pine or gnarled oak occupies what was the chimney nook, and a sweet-scented black-birch, perhaps, waves where the door-stone was. Sometimes the well dent is visible, where once a spring oozed; now dry and tearless grass; or it was covered deep, — not to be discovered till some late day, — with a flat stone under the sod, when the last of the race departed. What a sorrowful act must that be, — the covering up of wells! coincident with the opening of wells of tears. These cellar dents, like deserted fox burrows, old holes, are all that is left where once were the stir and bustle of human life,

Nature is one great theme of *Walden*, and the cycle of the seasons is the framework of the book. It begins in spring, goes through summer, fall, and winter, and ends in spring, with its "green, the symbol of perpetual youth." All the seasons are good: each "seems best to us in its turn."

Another great theme in *Walden* treats the independence of the individual human being. The situation of one man in a cabin in the woods suggests that theme. It is the Robinson Crusoe situation, of a man alone, having to make do with whatever he has. But the independence runs much deeper than that: it is an independence of the spirit, of being independent of false persuasions or groundless convention, of not doing what other people do just because they do it.

Thoreau meant to rouse his readers to throw off their false dependency. On the title page of our manuscript of *Walden*, he drew a sketch of a rooster and wrote under it that he hoped his book would wake his neighbors up. He said that "the mass of men lead lives of quiet desperation." That was his audience, the mass of men who "lead lives of quiet desperation." He tried to make them feel that they (or we) do not have to conform to what others do. "If a man does not keep pace with his companions, perhaps it is because he hears a different drummer. Let him step to the music which he hears, however measured or far away."

Thoreau felt that we are always running the risk of losing our independence.

> It is remarkable how easily and insensibly we fall into a particular route, and make a beaten track for ourselves. I had not lived there a week before my feet wore a path from my door to the pond-side; and though it is five or six years since I trod it, it is still quite distinct. It is true, I fear that others may have fallen into it, and so helped to keep it open. The surface of the earth is soft and impressible by the feet of men; and so with the paths which the mind travels. How worn and dusty, then, must be the highways of the world, how deep the ruts of tradition and conformity!

Being independent sometimes will get you in trouble, of course, and Thoreau's brush with the law led to what must be the best-publicized night any man ever spent in jail, with even a musical play having been written about it. When Thoreau visited Concord one day in July 1846—while he was living at Walden Pond—he was taken into custody by his friend Sam Staples, the constable, and put in jail for not paying his poll tax. He had refused to do so because he was unwilling to support a government that tolerated slavery. Thoreau told about his time in jail as follows: "I did not for a

181

moment feel confined, and the walls seemed a great waste of stone and mortar. I felt as if I alone of all my townsmen had paid my tax." There is a story, only perhaps true, that Emerson came to visit him in jail and asked him, "Why are you here?" Thoreau made exactly the right rejoinder when he replied, "Why are you not here?" The next morning, Thoreau was released from jail. Someone—perhaps his aunt—had paid his tax.

After two years, two months, and two days, Thoreau left Walden. In going through scraps of his manuscripts that seem to have been written during that period, I ran across one that contains a scribbled list of words, as follows: "Snow in Summer . . . Trivial . . . Perchance . . . seem have to . . . After all—in fact—indeed &c" Beside this scribble, he penciled in these momentous words: "Left Walden Woods Sep 6 1847." That was indeed the very day he left Walden to return to civilization, and I was holding in my hand the same piece of paper he had held on that day.

Why did he leave the woods? Why didn't he stay there for the rest of his life? He later confided his thoughts on this subject in his Journal, and they are revealing: "I do not think that I can tell," he wrote. "I have often wished myself back. . . . Perhaps I wanted a change. There was a little stagnation, it may be. . . . Perhaps if I lived there much longer, I might live there forever. One would think twice before he accepted heaven on such terms."

Anyway, Thoreau sold his cabin to Emerson's Irish gardener, who dug a cellar hole by it as part of a plan to enlarge it into a cottage for his family. But liquor spoiled his plans, and the cabin too. It fell into the cellar hole, and it was later hauled away and the timber used, ignominiously, for a pig pen, a stable shed, and patching for a barn.

When Thoreau returned to Concord, one of the tasks that fell to him was to answer a letter from the secretary of his Harvard class of 1837. They had been out for ten years, and the class secretary sent a questionnaire to accumulate data on the occasion of this anniversary. Thoreau tells about himself as follows:

"I confess that I have very little class spirit, and have almost forgotten that I ever spent four years at Cambridge. That must have been in a former state of existence. It is difficult to realize that the old routine is still kept up. However, I will undertake at last to answer your questions as well as I can in spite of a poor memory and a defect of information. . . .

"I dont know whether mine is a profession, or a trade, or what not. . . . I am a Schoolmaster—a Private Tutor, a Surveyor—a Gardener, a Farmer—a Painter, I mean a House Painter, a Carpenter, a Mason, a Day-Laborer, a Pencil-Maker, a Glass-paper Maker, a Writer, and sometimes a Poetaster. . . .

"For the last two or three years I have lived in Concord woods alone, something more than a mile from any neighbor, in a house built entirely by myself. . . .

"P.S. I beg that the Class will not consider me an object of charity, and if any of them are in want of pecuniary assistance, and will make known their case to me, I will engage to give them some advice of more worth than money."

There is no evidence that any classmate applied to him for "pecuniary assistance," but Thoreau proceeded to give them—and all the world—his "advice of more worth than money." He did it by writing *Walden*.

III

Thoreau spent about six years in writing and revising *Walden*, and it was published in Boston in 1854. Before submitting it for publication, he felt a little uneasy about the fate of his book, and for a reason that requires some explanation.

In 1849 he had published a book called *A Week on the Concord and Merrimack Rivers*, the story of a trip that he and his brother John took in New Hampshire, traveling in a homemade boat. *Walden* may give the impression that Thoreau never left home—one of its famous remarks is, "I have travelled a good deal in Concord." He did venture off a little, however. Once he took, with a friend, a ten-day excursion trip by train to Canada (total fare, $7), and wrote it up as a book known as *A Yankee in Canada;* the final version of our three manuscripts begins a follows: "I fear that I have not got much to say about Canada, not having seen much; what I got by going to Canada was a cold." For any book with such a beginning, it has to be downhill the rest of the way. (In the first version, the sentence

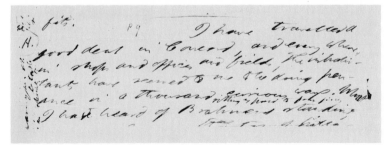

had wryly continued: ". . . a cold, which of course you do not wish me to communicate to you.") Thoreau took another trip also, to Minnesota. In rummaging through his loose papers about that trip, I ran across the following note in his handwriting: "Thursday put in wash 3 shirts, 1 flannel, 1 pr. drawers, 4 bosoms, 5 handkerchiefs (2 small cotton), 1 pair socks." From this record, I judge that he was pretty economical in his sock wearing, or else pretty liberal with shirts and handkerchiefs; and that he kept his notes.

But to get back to his book *A Week on the Concord and Merri-*

The Concord River near Concord. This picture is an 1869 photograph of a drawing by May Alcott.

mack Rivers. It was rejected by four publishers. The book was finally issued, but only after Thoreau had agreed to guarantee the printing costs, of some $290. It was unfavorably reviewed, and four years after publication, only 219 of the 1,000 copies had been sold and Thoreau had been credited with only $15 in royalties. The publisher got tired of holding all those books that wouldn't sell, and so he shipped the lot of them to Thoreau in Concord. Thoreau noted in his Journal: "I have now a library of nearly nine hundred volumes, over seven hundred of which I wrote myself." (And he added, doubt-less with a sly smile! "Is it not well that the author should behold the fruits of his labor? My works are piled up on one side of my chamber half as high as my head.")

In view of this experience, we can understand why Thoreau was uneasy about making arrangements for the publication of *Walden*. He had written a first draft of the new book while he was still living in the cabin at the pond, and before *A Week on the Concord and Merrimack Rivers* was published. The first draft was about half the length of *Walden* as we know it. Thoreau was deeply concerned that the book communicate his experiences and his thoughts fully and faithfully, and he spent about five years revising it. He went back to his Journal and his notes for passages and ideas, he tried out sections in public lectures, and he reorganized the parts. Always he was adjusting and perfecting the style: for example, a passage from the Journal that went, "I have travelled some in New England, especially in Concord," became the wry comment, "I have travelled a good deal in Concord." "The mass of mankind lead lives of quiet desperation" became, by one tiny but crucial change, "The mass of men lead lives of quiet desperation." And so it went, with careful attention to the language of each sentence.

In all, the manuscript of *Walden* at the Huntington consists of almost 1200 pages of Thoreau's writing, on many different kinds and sizes of paper, in ink and in pencil, with cancellations and with interlinear changes in profusion. Scholars have been able to trace seven different versions of *Walden* in this tangle of papers, and our appreciation of the book is increased by an understanding of the painstaking manner in which Thoreau created his masterpiece.

His uneasiness about the publication of his book was unfounded. It turned out that the first publisher he consulted—Ticknor and Fields, perhaps the leading publisher of the time—agreed to accept it. Moreover, they offered to publish it at their own expense and to give Thoreau a liberal royalty of fifteen percent of the list price. Thoreau was particular about his book right to the end. The corrected proofs (which are also at the Huntington) reveal his final care in polishing his language. For example, he wrote—and the printer

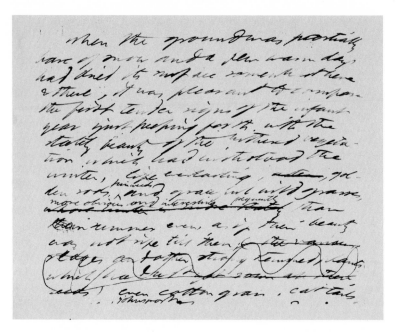

set—the phrase "to whomsoever does this work." It doubtless struck Thoreau as rough and awkward; instead of simply correcting the lapsed grammar, he revised it in proof to read "to him who does this work"—which is strong, straightforward Thoreau. He took pains also to revise his punctuation in the proofs; he added commas, for example, to set off expressions that would be more effective if marked for a pause in the reading.

The proofs also reveal the printer's difficulties with Thoreau's handwriting. At one point, the printer writes in the margin the plaintive cry, "Can't read the MS." In another place, "MS not legible." One phrase the printer had found illegible, he set as "these hearers"; Thoreau put it right, as "their Heaven."

On August 9, 1854, *Walden* was published at $1 a copy. (For the benefit of comparative shoppers, I will mention that Thoreau pencils, luxury items, sold for 75¢ a dozen.) On that same day, Thoreau made the following terse entry in his Journal: "To Boston. 'Walden' published. Elder-berries. Waxwork yellowing." That is his total entry for the day. To the end, books and elder-berries are on a par.

In the five-year period from 1850 to 1855—which included the publication of *Walden*—a remarkable number of other American books of the very first importance appeared: Hawthorne's *The Scarlet Letter* and *The House of the Seven Gables*, Melville's *Moby-Dick*,

Whitman's *Leaves of Grass*, Harriet Beecher Stowe's *Uncle Tom's Cabin*. And also many of the second rank, such as Longfellow's *Song of Hiawatha*, Emerson's *Representative Men*, and works of Whittier and Oliver Wendell Holmes. Even among this group of distinguished books, *Walden* takes a place of prime importance.

per to build the whole yourself than to
er of the advantage of the common wall;
have done this, the common partition, to
er, must be a thin one, and that other
ad neighbor, and also not keep his side in
only coöperation which is commonly pos-
lingly partial and superficial; and what
eration there is, is as if it were not, being
udible to men. If a man has faith he
with equal faith every where; if he has
ill continue to live like the rest of the
r company he is joined to. To coöperate,
as well as the lowest sense, means *to get*
her. I heard it proposed lately that two
ould travel together over the world, the
ney, earning his means as he went, before
behind the plough, the other carrying a
ge in his pocket. It was easy to see that
long be companions or coöperate, since
operate at all. They would part at the
crisis in their adventures. Above all,
lied, the man who goes alone can start
who travels with another must wait till
eady, and it may be a long time before

is very selfish, I have heard some of my
I confess that I have hitherto indulged
philanthropic enterprises. I have made
to a sense of duty, and among others
this pleasure also. There are those who
their arts to persuade me to undertake

the support of some poor family in the town; and if I had nothing to do,—for the devil finds employment for the idle,—I might try my hand at some such pastime as that. However, when I have thought to indulge myself in this respect, and lay these hearers under an obligation by maintaining certain poor persons in all respects as comfortably as I maintain myself, and have even ventured so far as to make them the offer, they have one and all unhesitatingly preferred to remain poor. While my townsmen and women are devoted in so many ways to the good of their fellows, I trust one at least may be spared to other and less humane pursuits. You must have a genius for charity as well as for any thing else. As for doing-good, that is one of the professions which are full. Moreover, I have tried it fairly, and, strange as it may seem, am satisfied that it does not agree with my constitution. Probably I should not consciously and deliberately forsake my particular calling to do the good which society demands of me, to save the universe from annihilation; and I believe that a like but infinitely greater steadfastness elsewhere is all that now preserves it. But I would not stand between any man and his genius; and to whomsoever does this work, which I decline, with his whole heart and soul and life, I would say, persevere, even if the world call it doing evil, as it is most likely they will.

I am far from supposing that my case is a peculiar one; no doubt many of my readers would make a similar defence. At doing something,—I will not engage that my neighbors shall pronounce it good,—I do not hesitate to say that I should be a capital fellow to hire; but what that is, it is for my employer to find out. What *good* I do in the common sense of that word must

MS. not legible

A proof sheet of *Walden,* with corrections by Thoreau. The three darker corrections (in ink, including "MS. not legible") are by the printer; the other corrections (in pencil) are all by Thoreau.

IV

Walden, as a book about nature, appeals to a dream of purity and innocence. "We can never have enough of Nature," wrote Thoreau. F. Scott Fitzgerald expressed the feeling of many of us in a letter to his daughter the year before he died: "After reading Thoreau I felt how much I have lost by leaving nature out of my life." *Walden* responds to our need for renewal and strength. The myth of nature is a nostalgic idea, in which picnics are not marred by mosquitoes or ants, and campers do not have to cope with torrential rains.

The myth of nature as primitive perfection is a usable ideal, and it is an important basis for living. It becomes operative as a model when the real possibility begins to recede into the past. Now we have deep concern for the deterioration of our environment, and many ecological movements try to protect what is left of it.

Thoreau was there before us. In his Journal he set forth plainly the views that *Walden* dramatizes. He said: "Most men; it seems to me, do not care for Nature and would sell their share in all her beauty . . . many for a glass of rum. Thank God, men cannot as yet fly, and lay waste the sky as well as the earth! We are safe on that side for the present. It is for the very reason that some do not care for those things that we need to continue to protect all from the vandalism of a few."

What prophetic words, more than a century ago! He went further, as a lover of nature, as a conservationist, and argued in his Journal that "each town should have a park, or rather primitive forest, of five hundred or a thousand acres, where a stick should never be cut for fuel, a common possession forever, for instruction and recreation. . . . As some give to Harvard College or another institution, why might not another give a forest or huckleberry-field to Concord." Emerson was right after all: Thoreau could be "captain of a huckleberry party." But he could be—and he was—a great deal more.

The other great theme of *Walden*—the independence of the individual human being—offers a goal toward which to strive, a model for the future. For Thoreau, this independence has to do with maintaining a sense of integrity in dealing with other people and with social and political institutions, like a government.

What Thoreau offers is strong medicine. *Walden* is a strong book because it is a deeply idealistic book. It is not for the squeamish—though you don't have to be able (like Thoreau) to "eat a fried rat with relish" in order to value it.

It is a book intended to stir people out of their lethargy. The generation gap, for example, is very explicit in *Walden.* "I have lived some thirty years on this planet," he wrote, "and I have yet to hear the first syllable of valuable or even earnest advice from my seniors."

He tries to move people away from our conventional job-centered world. The question, he wrote, is "how to get my living honestly, with freedom left for my proper pursuits."

The principle of freedom for the individual—so strong in the Declaration of Independence and in the first ten amendments to the Constitution—comes out in Thoreau's ideas about government. "There will never be a really free and enlightened State," he wrote, "until the State comes to recognize the individual as a higher and independent power, from which all its own power and authority are derived, and treats his accordingly."

In the spring of 1836, Thoreau had to withdraw from college for a term because of illness. It is probable that this illness was his first attack of tuberculosis, a disease which caused the death of a grandfather, a sister, a brother, and many other Concord residents. Thoreau suffered from tuberculosis through his mature years, and it is assumed that his life was prolonged by spending much of his time outdoors. On the other hand, a period of sitting in the snow to count the growth rings of some tree stumps hastened the progress of his final lingering illness. He died in May of 1862, at the age of forty-four, a person relatively unknown beyond the local circles of Concord.

Emerson delivered the address at the funeral service, and he published it three months later as an essay in the *Atlantic Monthly.* Emerson's working manuscript of his essay is at the Huntington, and a perusal of the detailed revisions shows the pains that the more distinguished man took in trying to give a faithful account of his younger friend, with whom he had been in close touch for the nearly twenty-five years since Thoreau graduated from college.

It is relatively easy to communicate facts about another person, harder to make a just balance of strengths and weaknesses, hardest of all to convey a deep sense of another human being. Emerson recognized Thoreau's sincere devotion to truth, his unswerving honesty, his idealistic love of nature. Emerson thought that his faults were virtues run to extremes: hence Thoreau's instinct to say No to propositions, his lack of affectionate relations, the absence of worldly ambition in him. But Thoreau had the wisdom of heavenly vision, Emerson thought, and the genius of his unsleeping insight revealed the material world as a means and symbol of perfection that is beyond human words.

Walden gives us a model for living in tune with the inner life of nature and at peace with the sense of our own integrity. This model, this dream, has a special appeal to us now because it touches our current needs and fears. If one were to ask whether this dream is at peace with the needs of society, one might allow Thoreau to answer in a parable. When he lay on his deathbed, an aunt asked him whether he had made his peace with God. Thoreau replied, "I did not know that we had ever quarreled."

Thoreau's cabin in the woods at Walden Pond. This picture is an 1869 photograph of a drawing by May Alcott.

Frontiersmen of the Spirit

FOUR MASTERS OF
TWENTIETH-CENTURY
LITERATURE

WILLIAM BUTLER YEATS

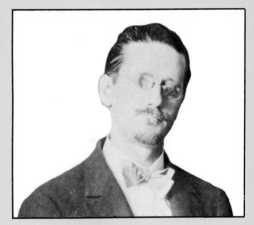

JAMES JOYCE

WALLACE STEVENS

CONRAD AIKEN

WHEN the first group of Puritans arrived in the area that we now call Boston, in 1630, they were astonished to find that an Englishman was there before them. The man was William Blackstone. In fact, he had been there for seven years, all by himself. He had bought the choicest land from the local Indians—including what is now the Boston Common and Beacon Hill—and he had built himself a house and planted an orchard and a garden. Mostly, however, he was busy reading, from his library of some two hundred volumes, and he loved the frontier life.

Blackstone was a graduate of Emmanuel College, Cambridge University, where he took the BA degree in 1617 and the MA in 1621. (He was at Emmanuel just one decade before John Harvard, who also went there, and who had a college named for him. Blackstone did not.) Although he had become a clergyman in the Church of England as soon as he graduated, he left his home country right away to avoid what he considered the repressive force of the church.

Blackstone was not a Puritan, however, and he was not pleased when the Puritans intruded on his frontier life in Boston. They came armed with a land grant from the king of England, and they set up a court and a church and a tax system. They squabbled about land ownership, and ultimately they got most of Blackstone's land.

For Blackstone, it was no longer the frontier. He preferred the Indians to the Bostonians, and in 1634 he moved along to a new frontier, what we call Rhode Island. There he became the first settler, as he had been the first settler of Boston. He said that he "came from England to get rid of the Lord Bishops" and that he left Boston "to get rid of the Lord Bretheren." In the new frontier of Rhode Island, he built a house and planted an orchard and a garden, and he devoted himself once more to his books.

This story about a somewhat mysterious person was very intriguing to Conrad Aiken. He said of Blackstone:

He is a tantalizing figure, in many respects the true prototypical American: ancestor alike of those pioneers who sought freedom and privacy in the 'wide open spaces,' or the physical conquest of an untamed continent, and those others, early and late, who were to struggle for it in the darker kingdoms of the soul. Daniel Boone and Johnny Appleseed were his grandchildren. But so too were Thoreau and Melville and Henry Adams. And the outlaws, the lone wolves, the lost souls, — yes, these as well.

Aiken wrote a long poem about William Blackstone and all of these descendants of his spirit. He called it *The Kid,* and he commenced writing it on the back flyleaf of a biography of Kit Carson—the copy is now in the Huntington Library—a book in which the author had maintained that "Kit Carson has become a symbol of the American frontier, as Odysseus was of the Greek seafarings, and it is important that we understand and love the thing he represents."

For Aiken, the frontier was not only the material world out there, the world of unpathed forests and raging rivers that have to be conquered. The frontier was also on the inside, our sense of human consciousness.

I am taking the legend of William Blackstone and the frontier of the spirit as a sort of parable. I want to use it to draw together four great masters of twentieth-century literature. They can be considered frontiersmen of the spirit in the sense that they were all concerned with our capacity for deeper awareness. Each of them tried, in his own way, to extend and refine that human capability.

All four men are prominently represented in the Exhibition Hall of the Library. Indeed, the last two displays, one British and one American, are devoted to their works. The British section features William Butler Yeats (whom many consider the most significant British poet so far in this century, who died in 1939) and James Joyce (who is often thought of as the most notable and influential British novelist of the century, who died in 1941). The American section features Wallace Stevens (whom many regard as the most important poet of our century, who died in 1955), and Conrad Aiken (who is perhaps our most wide-ranging man of letters of the century, who died in 1973).

The material on display is spectacular, but it represents only the tiniest fraction of our holdings. Ideally, that should always be true of what is behind the scenes in a research library, which tries to provide the richest possible reservoir of material for use by a wide variety of scholars for a multitude of purposes. Out of those holdings, an almost unlimited number of exhibitions can be prepared that will be interesting and rewarding to those of us who are not specialists in that particular field.

Our collection of the printed books of these four writers is essentially complete for all of them in all works of importance. We also have dazzling collections of their manuscripts, letters, and other unique materials. For Yeats, we have more than a hundred letters, as well as many other manuscripts and his own copy of his collected *Poems* (1899), with his full annotations and revisions. For Joyce, there are several hundred pages of manuscript material, including (for example) an important portion of his final revised typescript from which the printer set *Ulysses.*

194

For Stevens and Aiken, we have the best holdings in the world, including, for each of them, the writer's own archive of his manuscripts, notebooks, correspondence, library, and photographs. The collections are still growing as we continue to add to them from other sources; the Stevens manuscript collection now numbers nearly seven thousand items, that for Aiken more than four thousand, and they are rich in material for many related uses.

William Butler Yeats

II

I return to the question of the ways in which these four writers can be considered frontiersmen. The frontiersman, like William Blackstone, usually has some kind of dissatisfaction with the old order and a desire to change it. Persons of genius—which these four were—have the talent to take themselves, and us with them, into new territory.

For each of these four writers, I want to single out a few characteristic incidents from their lives. I also want to quote one or two typical passages from the writings of each of them in the hope of conveying the spirit of their accomplishments. This, their writing, is the heart of the matter. "My true self, my poems," wrote Yeats, and in this he can speak for all of them. I trust that it will become clear in what sense these notable writers changed our way of looking at the world.

William Butler Yeats started his life in Ireland in 1865 and lived mainly there. His father, John Butler Yeats, was a portrait painter, of limited success, as he could hardly bring himself to finish a portrait. He lavished attention on his eldest child William, whom he called Willie. Hour after hour he talked with him, or lectured to him, mainly on art and poetry, and he took him to visit friends, most of whom were writers and painters. Breakfast time was given over to the father reading aloud to the family; he specialized in the most passionate scenes from Shakespeare.

He felt concern for his son. "I am very anxious about Willie," he wrote to his wife, "he is never out of my thoughts. I believe him to be intensely affectionate, but from shyness, sensitiveness and nervousness, difficult to win and yet he is worth winning. I should of course like to see him do what is right but he will only develop by kindness and affection and gentleness."

From the son's point of view, it was not all gentleness, however. Here is his account of one episode with his father:

> One night a quarrel over **Ruskin came** to such a height that in putting me out of the room **he broke the** glass in a picture with the back of my head. **Another night when** we had been in argument over Ruskin or mysticism, I cannot now remember what theme, he followed me upstairs to the room I shared with my brother. He squared up at me, and wanted to box, and when I said I could not fight my own father replied, 'I don't see why you should not'. My brother, who had been in bed for some time, started up in a violent passion because we had awaked him. My father fled without speaking

It is probably not surprising that the father once complained to one of his daughters that "I wish Willie did not sometimes treat me as if I was a black beetle."

In 1908 his father went to New York with that same daughter, Lily, for a short visit. The daughter went home, but he did not. In fact the visit was prolonged for fourteen years, till he died in 1922. It was later that same year that the son was awarded the Nobel Prize for literature and became a senator for Ireland.

The son was a productive writer to the very end of his life. (And he continued to dream about his father, strange dreams in which the father sometimes appeared as the eyepiece of a telescope, and sometimes as a stool.) When he died, in 1939, he left behind what has long been thought of as some of the best of all English poetry.

Yeats had begun writing poems when he was young. His early poetry deals with escape from life into death. Here's the beginning of one of his young poems, a sentimental love song written in his twenties, of which we have a manuscript. In the poem, the young woman has grown old, the poet (the maker of a book of poems about her) is dead.

When you are old and grey and full of sleep
And nodding by the fire, take down this book,
And slowly read and dream of the soft look
Your eyes had once and of their shadows deep.

196

When you are old and grey and full of sleep
And nodding by the fire, take down this book,
And slowly read and dream of the soft look
your eyes had once and of their shadows deep;

I will arise and go now and go to the island
                    of Innisfree
And live in a dwelling of wattles – of woven
              wattles and woodwork made,
Nine been rows will I have there, a
          ^   yellow hive for the honey ^
                                    bee
And this old care shall fade.

In these early poems, Yeats sometimes seeks to escape to a garden on an island, a place where he will (like William Blackstone) be isolated from the rest of the world—including, I judge, from his father. Such as in his best-known early poem, "The Lake Isle of Innisfree," which begins in our manuscript version:

I will arise and go now and go to the island of Innisfree
And live in a dwelling of wattles, of woven wattles and
 wood-work made.
Nine bean-rows will I have there, a yellow hive for the honey-bee,
And this old care shall fade.

Thoreau's *Walden* was in Yeats's mind when he wrote this poem. Thoreau had isolated himself at Walden Pond, and Yeats imagined himself on a garden island of the mind in his search for wisdom.

The nature of Yeats's poetry kept changing throughout his life. He was also one of the world's greatest revisers: his own copy of his *Collected Poems* of 1899—now at the Huntington—shows the way he rewrote much of it. To those who complained about his habit of revising, he penned the following verses:

The friends that have it I do wrong
When ever I remake a song,
Should know what issue is at stake:
It is myself that I remake.

As a fine example of Yeats, I would like to quote one of his later poems entitled "Sailing to Byzantium." He is a frontiersman, on the move, breaking new ground. This time he is moving—sailing —from the natural world of the body, in which people grow old, to the world of art, which is timeless. There you leave your natural form behind and take on any shape you like, that of a golden bird, say. The name Byzantium is, literally, the earlier name for Constantinople; but Yeats uses it to mean eternity.

I hope that you will read this poem aloud. Much of its effect comes from the music of the verse and from its dramatic spirit. Usually it takes several readings to feel that you have gotten the emphasis on the right words and have hit the right tone. But the reward, of feeling that you have really responded to the poem, is very great. Here is the poem, as it first appeared in print, in a book from the Cuala Press published in Dublin in 1927 by Yeats's younger sister:

SAILING TO BYZANTIUM

I

That is no country for old men. The young
In one another's arms, birds in the trees—
Those dying generations — at their song,
The salmon-falls, the mackerel-crowded seas,
Fish flesh or fowl, commend all summer long
Whatever is begotten born and dies.
Caught in that sensual music all neglect
Monuments of unageing intellect.

II

An aged man is but a paltry thing,
A tattered coat upon a stick, unless
Soul clap its hands and sing, and louder sing
For every tatter in its mortal dress,
Nor is there singing school but studying
Monuments of its own magnificence;
And therefore I have sailed the seas and come
To the holy city of Byzantium.

III

O sages standing in God's holy fire
As in the gold mosaic of a wall,
Come from the holy fire, perne in a gyre,
And be the singing masters of my soul.
Consume my heart away; sick with desire
And fastened to this dying animal
It knows not what it is; and gather me
Into the artifice of eternity.

IV

Once out of nature I shall never take
My bodily form from any natural thing,
But such a form as Grecian goldsmiths make
Of hammered gold and gold enamelling
To keep a drowsy emperor awake;
Or set upon a golden bough to sing
To lords and ladies of Byzantium
Of what is past, or passing, or to come.

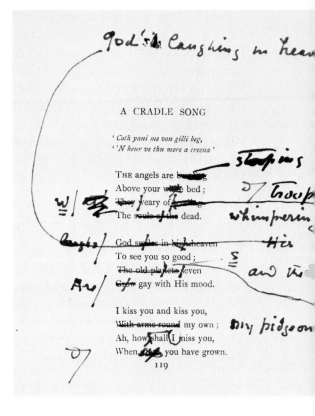

A page from Yeats's Poems (1899), showing his revisions of one poem for a new edition.

A CRADLE SONG

' *Coth yani me von gilli beg,*
'' '*N heur ve thu more a creena* '

THE angels are ~~bending~~
Above your ~~white~~ bed ;
~~They weary of~~
The ~~souls of the~~ dead.

God ~~smiles in high heaven~~
To see you so good ;
~~The old planets seven~~
~~Grow~~ gay with His mood.

I kiss you and kiss you,
~~With arms round~~ my own ;
Ah, how shall I miss you,
When ~~that~~ you have grown.

119

James Joyce

III

When Yeats's play *The Countess Cathleen* was first produced, in 1899, in Dublin, it drew a great crowd. Many came because Yeats was already, at thirty-four, the principal living Irish writer, others because they had heard that the play was anti-Irish and heretical. James Joyce, age seventeen, was there among a crowd of fellow university students. His friends booed and hissed at its supposed anti-Irish views; Joyce clapped vigorously. They wrote a letter of protest for publication in a newspaper; Joyce refused to sign.

Three years later, Joyce first met Yeats in person, one evening in a restaurant in Dublin, and Joyce read some of his current writing to Yeats. Here is the way that Yeats remembered the occasion:

> [Joyce] read me a beautiful though immature and eccentric harmony of little prose descriptions and meditations. He had

200

thrown over metrical form, he said, that he might get a form so fluent that it would respond to the motions of the spirit. I praised his work but he said, "I really don't care whether you like what I am doing or not. It won't make the least difference to me. Indeed I don't know why I am reading to you."

Then, putting down his book, he began to explain all his objections to everything I had ever done. Why had I concerned myself with politics, with folklore, with the historical setting of events and so on? Above all why had I written about ideas, why had I condescended to make generalizations? These things were all the sign of the cooling of the iron, of the fading out of inspiration. . . .

Presently he got up to go, and, as he was going out, he said, "I am twenty. How old are you?" I told him, but I am afraid I said I was a year younger than I am. He said with a sigh, "I thought as much. I have met you too late. You are too old."

The gap between twenty and thirty-six (thirty-seven) was too much for one with Joyce's spirit. In the same year, when he was twenty, he decided to leave Ireland. He turned his back on his Jesuit education, on the Roman Catholic religion, even on Ireland itself. He went through London, where he spent only one day. He spent it in the company of William Butler Yeats. Yeats set his alarm, went to the station to meet Joyce's train at six o'clock in the morning, and spent the day introducing him to people who might be helpful to a beginning writer. That evening Joyce left for Paris and his self-imposed exile. He thought of himself as an exile, in search of a new frontier.

James Joyce with Sylvia Beach, the publisher of Ulysses, *in her Paris office.*

Joyce's final typescript for the opening of the last episode of Ulysses. *The printer set the first edition from this copy, which shows Joyce's handwritten corrections.*

Though he made several visits back to Ireland, most of the remainder of his life—from 1902 to 1941—was spent in Europe: mainly Paris, Trieste, Rome, and Zurich. Always writing, writing, writing. His two great masterpieces are, of course, the novels *Ulysses* and *Finnegans Wake.* Through all of Joyce's writings the setting is the Ireland of his youth. Though self-exiled, he was always in Ireland. In his writings, he was obsessed with getting the details of his Irish settings right, including the particulars about streets and houses. In *Ulysses,* for example, he tells of a character lowering himself "to within two feet ten inches of the area pavement" and then dropping to the ground without hurting himself. In order to be sure that he had gotten it right, however, he wrote to an aunt in Dublin and put this question:

Is it possible for an ordinary person to climb over the area railings of no 7 Eccles street, either from the path or the steps, lower himself down from the lowest part of the railings till his feet are within 2 feet or 3 of the ground and drop unhurt. I saw it done myself but by a man of rather athletic build. I require this information in detail in order to determine the wording of a paragraph.

I would like to take *Ulysses* as our sample of Joyce's work. It displays the frontier spirit I've been talking about both in its general situation and in its advance into new territory in the use of language.

The general situation in *Ulysses* is that the main characters are outcasts within their society, and in desperate search of something to give them a sense of fulfillment. Leopold Bloom, the hero, is a Jew in the Roman Catholic world of Dublin. He is regarded as an alien by the others, and (because he has renounced his own religion) is an outcast even in the eyes of Jews. He is a failure in his family, and he is thus alienated from country and religion and family life. His wife is Molly Bloom, who is unfaithful to him and amoral.

The novel is made up of eighteen episodes, which tell the story of Bloom's life on one day, June 16, 1904. The episodes are intricately related by their parallels to episodes in the *Odyssey*, the adventurous travels of Ulysses from the fall of Troy to his reunion at home with his faithful wife Penelope. Each of the episodes in Joyce's *Ulysses* has a different scene, a time, a symbol, and is set forth in one characteristic technique. Each also represents an organ of the body, an art, and a color.

Ulysses is a remarkable accomplishment, perhaps the most influential novel that has ever been published. No one part of it is characteristic of the whole, but I would like to focus attention on the passage with which the novel concludes. We have the final version of the manuscript for part of this concluding chapter in the Library, the very copy from which the printer worked when *Ulysses* was first set into type and printed; the beginning of this chapter is, in fact, on display in the Exhibition Hall.

This last episode, originally called Penelope, is an interior monologue of what is going through the head of Molly Bloom—modeled ironically on Penelope, wife of Ulysses—while she is lying in bed, late at night, going to sleep. It is a sample of the stream of consciousness that tries to represent the workings of the human mind as it moves back and forth in time and place, as it changes direction by association. This episode has had a profound influence on most later writers of fiction. It is without punctuation, and the episode runs to forty or fifty pages in most editions.

In the part I ask you to read, —in effect, the last page of the book—Molly is thinking about the time she got Leopold Bloom, her husband, to propose to her. Her monologue mingles the actions and thoughts that took place then, before then, and since then. The repetitions of the word *yes* are a kind of chorus in undertone, an epitome of Molly, and a foreshadowing of the conclusion.

The impact of the passage is very much truer to what Joyce intended if you read it aloud. Molly's nature and the way she thinks come out in the rhythms of the passage. Almost everyone's first experience, in trying to read it aloud, is puzzlement: it is difficult to sort out the shifts between inner thought and outside speaker, between the past and the present; but as these shifts become clear, the words can be given the emphasis they need in order to create the effect Joyce wanted us to feel. Here is the passage:

the sun shines for you he said the day we were lyin
among the rhododendrons on Howth head in the grey tweed suit and hi
straw hat the day I got him to propose to me yes first I gave him the bit c
seedcake out of my mouth and it was leapyear like now yes 16 years ag
my God after that long kiss I near lost my breath yes he said I was a flowe
of the mountain yes so we are flowers all a womans body yes that was on
true thing he said in his life and the sun shines for you today yes that wa
why I liked him because I saw he understood or felt what a woman is an
I knew I could always get round him and I gave him all the pleasure I coul
leading him on till he asked me to say yes and I wouldnt answer first onl
looked out over the sea and the sky I was thinking of so many things h
didnt know of Mulvey and Mr Stanhope and Hester and father and old captai
Groves and the sailors playing all birds fly and I say stoop and washing u
dishes they called it on the pier and the sentry in front of the governors hous
with the thing round his white helmet poor devil half roasted and the Spanis
girls laughing in their shawls and their tall combs and the auctions in th
morning the Greeks and the jews and the Arabs and the devil knows wh
else from all the ends of Europe and Duke street and the fowl market al
clucking outside Larby Sharons and the poor donkeys slipping half aslee
and the vague fellows in the cloaks asleep in the shade on the steps and th
big wheels of the carts of the bulls and the old castle thousands of years ol
yes and those handsome Moors all in white and turbans like kings asking yo
to sit down in their little bit of a shop and Ronda with the old window
of the posadas glancing eyes a lattice hid for her lover to kiss the iron an
the wineshops half open at night and the castanets and the night we misse
the boat at Algeciras the watchman going about serene with his lamp and C
that awful deepdown torrent O and the sea the sea crimson sometimes lik
fire and the glorious sunsets and the figtrees in the Alameda gardens ye
and all the queer little streets and pink and blue and yellow houses an
the rosegardens and the jessamine and geraniums and cactuses and Gibralta
as a girl where I was a Flower of the mountain yes when I put the rose i
my hair like the Andalusian girls used or shall I wear a red yes and how h
kissed me under the Moorish wall and I thought well as well him as anothe
and then I asked him with my eyes to ask again yes and then he asked m
would I yes to say yes my mountain flower and first I put my arms aroun
him yes and drew him down to me so he could feel my breasts all perfum
yes and his heart was going like mad and yes I said yes I will Yes.

Wallace Stevens

IV

Ulysses was first published in Paris in 1922, on James Joyce's fortieth birthday, February 2. A thousand copies were printed, each of them numbered, on several different kinds of paper. The Huntington Library has four copies: No. 56 (a presentation copy, signed by Joyce), No. 79 (another copy signed by Joyce), No. 122, and No. 466. Copy No. 466, the one on exhibition, is a notable copy: it was owned by Wallace Stevens. And that is the copy from which the passage you have just read was reproduced.

Stevens got his copy soon after publication by asking a friend to bring it back from Paris. "Smuggle" might be the better way to say it, as *Ulysses* was prohibited in the United States until 1933, until about the same time that the prohibition against alcoholic beverages was repealed—though there was no necessary connection between the two prohibitions. Stevens did ask his friend to bring —or smuggle—along with *Ulysses,* some liqueur from Santa Maria Novella, which was used for a celebration. Stevens also got a copy of Joyce's *Finnegans Wake* when it was published, and we have that copy too. It's not certain that he read either book, however, as they seem not to have been opened. Stevens can't be entirely blamed if he didn't read *Finnegans Wake,* since that book is often considered the most difficult work in the English language. Not that Stevens was unfamiliar with difficulty: some people think of him as the most difficult of all major poets in English.

On the face of it, Joyce and Stevens seem to be poles apart. Joyce lived as a self-imposed exile, and he was somewhat unconventional: he did not believe in marriage, for example, though the year before his first grandchild was born he and his wife were married at a registry office, "for testamentary reasons," as he said.

Stevens, on the other hand, lived a highly conventional life. Born in Reading, Pennsylvania, in 1879, the son of an attorney, he went to Harvard and the New York Law School, was admitted to the bar in 1904, married his hometown sweetheart, joined the legal staff of the Hartford Accident and Indemnity Company in 1916, rose to vice president in charge of bond claims in 1934, and worked hard at his insurance business until he died, in 1955, just short of the age of 76. Earlier he had said, "I shall be 75 next October and intend to stay 75 for some years after that."

Stevens was deeply interested in European writers and artists, but he never went to Europe. Indeed he hardly left home except on business or to take a long solitary walk. When he was young, he wrote to his fiancée (in a fit of irritation at living in New York) that "if things do not go well soon, I'll pack up and go to California or some other outlandish place." He did make a couple of brief visits to Havana, and in 1923 he and Mrs. Stevens went, by way of the Panama Canal, to California; they stopped in Pasadena at a hotel, and he recalled (more than twenty years later, and with some

This early poem by Stevens, in his own handwriting, is from a notebook which he gave, in June 1908, to Elsie Viola Moll. They were married in 1909.

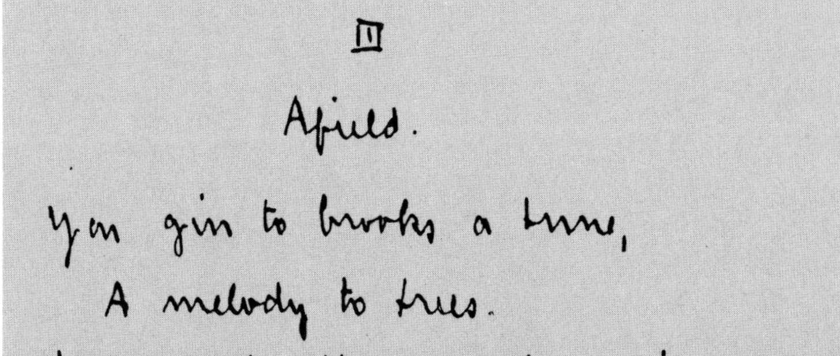

Ⅱ

Afield.

You give to brooks a tune,
   A melody to trees.
You make the dumb field sing aloud
   Its hidden harmonies.

An echo's murmur waits
   A little while and then
I hear the water and the pine
Take up their airs again.

inaccuracy) that "one of the Duveens was stopping at that particular hotel. It turned out afterwards that he had taken THE BLUE BOY out to show it to Mr. Huntington, who then bought it."

Stevens may not have traveled much, but he was a frontiersman all the same. Thoreau said of himself: "I have travelled a good deal in Concord." Stevens' principal life was lived inside himself. One of his aphorisms was, "We live in the mind."

He observed the world with care, and this vivid bit of imagery, from his private journal, is a fair sample of what he observed and how he recorded it: "Saw a child eating melting ice-cream from a paper and trying to pick up the drops on the pavement with its fingers." He absorbed the images into his mind, where they became a part of the reality of poetry, or the poetry of reality.

I put it both ways because one of the central problems or puzzles or mysteries for Stevens was how to break through the frontier of the limits of our understanding. "If it should be true," Stevens begins one section of his long poem called "An Ordinary Evening in New Haven," "If it should be true that reality exists / In the mind. . . ." And he goes on to ask whether, finally, the theory of poetry is or is not really the theory of life. Poetry was of vital significance to Stevens because it seemed to him crucial to that final belief, that supreme fiction, through which man may or can or may not find fulfillment.

Stevens kept his poetry and his insurance business separate. He rarely gave readings of his poetry, or talks. He avoided gatherings of writers and artists, though he delighted in corresponding with them. (Hence the best of his expressive self is probably in our collection of his papers.) He was a loner, in that American tradition of loners that Aiken talked about—a tradition that included Thoreau, Melville, Hawthorne, Emily Dickinson, Henry Adams, and the rest. One true image of him might be that of a solitary figure walking the two miles from his home in Hartford, by way of Elizabeth Park, to his insurance office. He was thinking, meditating, composing as he went along. Alone, but with much internal company.

Few were aware of the scope of his inner life. A visiting insurance man was startled to learn that Wallace Stevens wrote poetry. "What!" he exlaimed. "Wally a poet?"

He was a poet indeed, and a poet of the first magnitude. He began early and produced all his life, even getting better and better as he grew older. He did not publish his first volume, *Harmonium*, until he was forty-three years old, and the second volume had to wait till he was fifty-six. After that, the books came steadily for twenty years. He was more and more recognized, winning the Pulitzer Prize, the Bollingen Prize, and the National Book Award two times.

"One true image of him might be that of a solitary figure walking . . ."

Here is a single poem by Stevens in which the matters I have been speaking of may be evident. It is called "The World As Meditation." It tells a loving story about Penelope waiting patiently, faithfully, for the return of her husband Ulysses. She thinks of how she has prepared for him and what his return will be like; through her meditation on these particular things, she has created a reality about herself and her husband. The poem is also about the rising of the life-giving sun, and its shining on her pillow. But this poem — one of Stevens's last poems, and of the highest quality — also conveys a deep sense of the ultimate relationship of love as it can exist in the human spirit, through the reality of the human mind, even with all of the uncertainties that cloud our understanding.

This is another poem that gains from being read aloud, with careful emphasis on a lot of key words. The excitement through most of the poem calls for a fast pace, while the latter part becomes deliberate and grave. Here is the poem, reproduced from Stevens's own copy of the *Hudson Review* for 1952, where it first appeared in print:

The World as Meditation

Is it Ulysses that approaches from the east,
The interminable adventurer? The trees are mended.
That winter is washed away. Someone is moving

On the horizon and lifting himself up above it.
A form of fire approaches the cretonnes of Penelope,
Whose mere savage presence awakens the world in which she
    dwells.

She has composed, so long, a self with which to welcome him,
Companion to his self for her, which she imagined,
Two in a deep-founded sheltering, friend and dear friend.

The trees had been mended, as an essential exercise
In an inhuman meditation, larger than her own.
No winds like dogs watched over her at night.

She wanted nothing he could not bring her by coming alone.
She wanted no fetchings. His arms would be her necklace.
And her belt, the final fortune of their desire.

But was it Ulysses? Or was it only the warmth of the sun
On her pillow? The thought kept beating in her like her heart.
The two kept beating together.   It was only day.

It was Ulysses and it was not. Yet they had met,
Friend and dear friend and a planet's encouragement.
The barbarous strength within her would never fail.

She would talk a little to herself as she combed her hair,
Repeating his name with its patient syllables,
Never forgetting him that kept coming constantly so near.

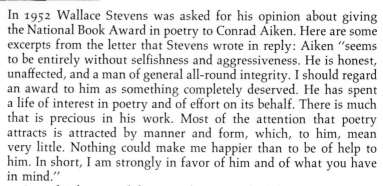

V

In 1952 Wallace Stevens was asked for his opinion about giving the National Book Award in poetry to Conrad Aiken. Here are some excerpts from the letter that Stevens wrote in reply: Aiken "seems to be entirely without selfishness and aggressiveness. He is honest, unaffected, and a man of general all-round integrity. I should regard an award to him as something completely deserved. He has spent a life of interest in poetry and of effort on its behalf. There is much that is precious in his work. Most of the attention that poetry attracts is attracted by manner and form, which, to him, mean very little. Nothing could make me happier than to be of help to him. In short, I am strongly in favor of him and of what you have in mind."

Conrad Aiken was duly given the National Book Award in poetry in 1953. Prizes were no novelty to him, actually, as he had won others, including the Pulitzer Prize for poetry in 1930. He was a prolific writer. In his career, he published some forty-two volumes, including five novels, several volumes of short stories, a play, a couple of volumes of critical essays, many volumes of poems, and some that are hard to classify. *The Coming Forth by Day of Osiris Jones*, for example. This is a grave-book inventory in verse of the sayings, acts, and deeds of ordinary men; it is the book that James Joyce, when he was blind and dying, kept asking to have bought for him.

In these forty-two volumes, there is much of permanent value because Conrad Aiken, too, was a frontiersman and these are the records of his explorations. Like William Blackstone, like the great Americans in *The Kid*, he was not content to follow in the tracks of other people. In fact, Aiken's discovery of the story of William Blackstone had an important influence on him, and the Blackstone legend planted many seeds in him.

Aiken was born in Savannah, Georgia, in 1889, the son of a prominent physician and surgeon. An event of the deepest significance occurred in his home when he was eleven years old. He awakened one February morning to the sound of his mother and father quarreling in their bedroom. He heard his father count "One, two, three," and then he heard two pistol shots. Young Conrad got up, walked through the bedroom of his three younger siblings and into his parents' room. They were both lying on the floor, dead: his father had shot his mother and then himself. Conrad shut the

Conrad Aiken at work in his Cape Cod home. Looking over his shoulder is Mrs. Aiken (the painter, Mary Augusta Hoover).

door, told his siblings to stay in bed, dressed and went downstairs, told the cook that there had been an accident and to see to the children and give them breakfast, and walked to the police station. There he reported that his father had shot his mother and himself. "Who is your father?" they asked. "Dr. Aiken," he replied.

The family was broken up, and the youngsters were sent to live with relatives. In due course, Aiken went to Harvard, where he was an undergraduate from 1907 to 1911. His fellow students included T.S. Eliot, Walter Lippmann, E. E. Cummings, and Robert Benchley, and T.S. Eliot became a close and lifelong friend. Aiken was elected Class Poet. Unfortunately the duties of that office involved a public performance at graduation. Aiken could not face such an ordeal, and he resigned from Harvard in the spring of his senior year to avoid it. (He did return the next year, however, and completed his work and took his degree when no public ceremony was required.)

I have mentioned that Wallace Stevens tried to avoid gatherings of writers, speeches, and the like. But he found it possible to take part on some occasions. He received a number of honorary degrees, for example, including one from Yale, which he (as a Harvard man) accepted with grace. Conrad Aiken found it impossible to do any of these things. When he was offered an honorary degree by Harvard in 1961, he declined; he wrote the president of Harvard of his "life-long horror of public appearances. It cyant be did. Bad enough when I was young—it prevented me from staying at

Harvard, the year after we met, because I was asked to give a lecture course, and knew I couldn't lecture—it's far worse now. An affliction, and I know I should be ashamed. Please forgive me, and ask the Governing Boards to forgive me."

The affliction didn't hinder him in his relations with individuals. He was a great friend, a great correspondent, a great human support, and a great influence on many people. The best record of this inner part of Aiken's life—as of Wallace Stevens's—is in the Huntington collections. Conrad Aiken's friendship with T.S. Eliot, for example, lasted for almost fifty years, the rest of Eliot's life, and it was very important to both of them. They exchanged poems, they talked about the problems of language, and Aiken carried Eliot's first major poem, "The Love Song of J. Alfred Prufrock," around with him until he could interest someone in publishing it. There are sixty-five valuable letters from Eliot to Aiken in our collection.

Conrad Aiken lived about equally in England and Georgia and New England. He always had the sense of uprootedness, of being a foreigner wherever he was. Yeats tried to solve this sense by submerging himself in folk myth and magic, Joyce by leaving home and writing about nothing except home, Stevens by living an almost entirely inner life. Aiken tried to solve it by deep analysis: he immersed himself in psychoanalytic writings, beginning when he was an undergraduate; and he tried to come to a complete understanding of himself, his motives, and his feelings—and to give expression to that understanding in words. In one way, all four of our authors were trying to do this same thing, James Joyce in particular. Conrad Aiken may have come closer than all the rest of them.

Freud offered to analyze Aiken. After thought and advice, Aiken decided against it. He suffered a lot of pain through his life, including that from his recurrent dreams. He tried to come to terms with them by putting them into exact words. Here is his own description of one, which he called "the execution dream," in which he found himself

> waiting in the chair for the onset of the electricity, then its profound assault on one's throat and breast and heart, fluctuatingly intrusive, but not at first intrusive enough, so that although one knew that one was dying, and tried to cry out an appeal for a deeper and more final intrusion, one succeeded only in a murmur so faint that no one heard it, and one's dying thought was "even in death I cannot be effectual, or make myself understood"

Actually, Aiken was notably effectual in making himself understood, within the limits of language. One of his great accomplishments as a writer was his success in breaking a barrier to inner understanding. He crossed a frontier by learning how to feel and to express his deepest thoughts with the shades and delicacy and grace that they made possible.

I conclude my remarks on Aiken with a passage from *Ushant* —reproduced from his own copy of that remarkable autobiography, first published in 1952—a book which is a great achievement in the expression of inner understanding. The story of Aiken's inner life is told mostly in the third person, as if it were about somebody else. In this passage, Aiken is trying to set forth his consciousness of that occasion, at the age of eleven, when he found his parents dead. It is a passage which should be read aloud, with pauses and emphasis, so that the delicate expression of deep emotion can be heard and felt.

the final scene of all: when, after the desultory early-morning quarrel, came the half-stifled scream, and then the sound of his father's voice counting three, and the two loud pistol-shots; and he had tiptoed into the dark room, where the two bodies lay motionless, and apart, and, finding them dead, found himself possessed of them forever. He had kept all this, on the one hand, in obeying the precept of the two lines of verse, and all the *modus vivendi* that it still represented, as in an album of faded photographs. But, also, even as he looked back at these, and at their immobility, as of artifact, he knew that he was irrevocably dedicated to a lifelong — if need be — search for an equivalent to it all, in terms of his own life, or work; and an equivalent that those two angelic people would have thought acceptable.

VI

All four of these writers are sometimes difficult to understand. Yeats wrote a poem, fairly early in his career, entitled "The Fascination of What's Difficult." In the twentieth century, particularly, the most original work in all of the arts—including painting, music, sculpture, and architecture, as well as literature—has been difficult on first contact. It may be that we always have an initial difficulty

213

with what is original, because it is, by its nature, outside of our normal experience up to that time. Moreover, we may be trying to "understand" with a vocabulary that doesn't yet have words to fit the new work.

The originality of Yeats and Joyce and Stevens and Aiken has to do with what I began by calling their role as frontiersmen of the spirit. Each of them tried to develop a deeper sense of human consciousness, and each of them had to develop and master a new form of expression—a new language, really—in order to communicate that sense of consciousness to others through his writings.

The writings of Yeats and Joyce and Stevens and Aiken have belonged to us for quite a while now. They have given us a deeper awareness of ourselves and of the human spirit. These four writers are true masters of twentieth-century literature.

*